EXPLORING MACHINES, BUILDINGS & WEAPONRY

OF BIBLICAL TIMES

2ND EDITION

MAX SCHWARTZ

First published under the title Machines, Buildings, and Weaponry of Biblical Times
by Wm. B. Eerdmans Publishing Co. 255 Jefferson Ave. S.E., Grand Rapids, MI 49503 /
P.O. Box 163, Cambridge CB3 9PU U.K.

This edition published 2003 by World Bible Publishers, Inc. Iowa Falls, IA 50126

03 04 05 06 07 PC 7 6 5 4 3 2 1

ISBN 0-529-11794-0

Contents

Preface

ON THE STAGE OF THE ANCIENT HOLY LAND, EARLY CIVILIZATIONS
played out the drama of history as they came to power, ruled, and
disappeared. The Bible records many of the events of these powerful
empires—but we may not recognize how this panoply was shaped by
behind-the-scenes influences and dramatic innovations in science, engineering, and warfare.

All the great powers that conquered the ancient Middle East relied on
newly acquired technical knowledge to build their great palaces, fortresses,
tombs, water and sanitation systems, transportation systems, and weapons
of war. These tools helped maintain these societies.

Exploring Machines, Buildings, Weaponry of Biblical Times focuses
on the history of the ancient science of engineering, which reached new
peaks with every successive empire that ruled the Middle East—
Egyptian, Assyrian, Babylonian, Persian, Greek, and Roman. Using the
Bible as a major source and including evidence from archaeological finds
and ancient texts, I have sought to show the interaction between engineering and the biblical world.

By *biblical world,* I mean the Middle East and eastern Mediterranean
region during the time of the events recorded in the Old and New
Testaments. The Bible speaks of engineering as early as Genesis, where
God told Noah how to build the ark:

> *Make a boat from resinous wood, sealing it with tar; and construct decks
> and stalls throughout the ship. Make it 450 feet long, 75 feet wide, and 45
> feet high. Construct a skylight all the way around the ship, eighteen
> inches below the roof; and make three decks inside the boat-a bottom,
> middle, and upper deck-and put a door in the side.* Genesis 6:14-16 TLB

The "Tower of Babel," the Tabernacle, the walls of Jericho, Hezekiah's water tunnel—the pages of the Bible are filled with engineering. This book will consider some of these things, as well as extra-biblical advances in science and engineering during the biblical period. Historians differ on the exact dating, but for our purposes we will consider that the biblical period began about 1682 B.C., the time of Abraham, and continued through the end of the Roman period, about A.D. 324.

My writing springs from a lifelong association with architecture and military and civil engineering. Though my first love has always been architectural history, I became a civil engineer after a stint with the United States Army Corps of Engineers and enrollment in the University of Southern California School of Engineering.

But this book also is a cultural and spiritual exploration by a Jew searching for his past. I have sought to relate my educational, spiritual, and professional life experiences to those of my ancient and biblical counterparts. Although I examine the biblical period, I do not try to prove or disprove any aspect of the Bible. I only intend to interpret the past, to shed more light on history, and to provide a clearer understanding of the state of engineering knowledge in the ancient world. In this way, I hope the reader can gain new insight into the Bible.

List of Illustrations

1

The Ancient Engineer

IN BIBLICAL TIMES, MASSIVE CONSTRUCTION PROJECTS REQUIRED complex masonry works, the moving of heavy stones, and some intricate mathematics. Then, as now, engineers needed great skill and knowledge to perform their tasks well.

Our word *engineer* comes from the Latin *ingeniator*, which described those who built engines of war. Throughout history, the military has been responsible for training and employing most engineers—even though these people have worked on many "civil" projects, such as roads, bridges, and harbors. Not until the eighteenth century did engineering become a distinctly civilian profession. Even in American history, we find the United States Army Corps of Engineers responsible for many structures and passageways used by the general population. In the same way, most major engineering works of ancient times—the aqueducts, drainage systems, harbors, highways, and public buildings—were government financed, designed by military engineers, and constructed by soldiers or captive laborers.

In ancient military history, just as in modern military practices, when a new weapon of war was introduced, the opposing power invented a counter weapon for defense. For example, the fort was perhaps the first "war machine," built to defend a settlement from being overrun by its enemies. Initially, fortresses had to provide defense against climbing soldiers and flying arrows and spears. So the earliest military engineers built high masonry walls with protective moats and *glacis* (sloped embankments) outside the walls. These defensive innovations forced attackers to develop tall, wooden, hide-covered siege towers that would reach the top of the walls and protect the soldiers who pounded the walls below with battering ram. This invention, in turn, made new defensive machinery necessary.

My research in writing this book led me back to the preceding civilizations in Western Asia. Each society inherited technical knowledge and skills from their predecessors. I followed the *Fertile Crescent* from where Abraham led the ancient Jewish people from the city of Ur on the Persian Gulf to the Holy Land, with stops at Babylon, Mari, Haran, Damascus, Jerusalem, and Beersheba.

Between 6000-5000 B.C., only isolated villages and farmers existed in the Middle East until the *Akkadians* and *Sumerians* took control of the land. A thousand years later, between 4000-3500 B.C., the Babylonians conquered the area and absorbed knowledge of the previous cultures. They continued their conquest westward around the *Fertile Crescent* to absorb Judea and Canaan, exiling the defeated Jews back to Babylon. This brutal rule finally ended when Persian armies defeated the Babylonians and permitted the Jews to return to the Holy Land and rebuild their Temple. The post-exilic Jews brought with them many technical skills from the Persians. Meanwhile, to the south, Egyptian civilization continued to thrive from 3500-1500 B.C.

There followed a sequence of invading armies and their subsequent defeats until in 70 B.C., when the Romans defeated the Jews and brought full Roman control over the Holy Land.

Roman Engineers

The Romans, civilization's great borrowers, made the most of their knowledge of others. They learned their basic engineering skills from the *Etruscans*, who had ruled the Italian peninsula for at least three hundred years before them. As the Romans extended their rule throughout the Mediterranean, they gained more engineering knowledge from the Greeks and from Middle Eastern cultures.

They put all this to good use in developing a civilian infrastructure. Once the empire was established and Rome could enjoy the lengthy *Pax Romana*, Roman military engineers turned their attention to roads, bridges, and public buildings. These would enhance Rome's control of its occupied territories and put a distinctly Roman stamp on the whole Mediterranean world.

As in other historical periods of great building projects, the engineer or architect (the two terms in Latin were virtually interchangeable) was a celebrated member of society—someone who had to have expertise in many areas. First-century Roman engineer and philosopher *Vitruvius* described the kind of person the job required:

- *He must be literate and able to express himself clearly.*

- *He must be a skilled draughtsman and capable of drawing plans, elevations, and renderings in perspective sketches.*

- *He must be a mathematician, as well as competent in geometric construction and arithmetic.*

- *He must have an encyclopedic knowledge of mythology and legend, to plan pedimental sculptures or friezes.*

- *He must be familiar with several branches of philosophy.*

- *He must understand the basics of acoustic and musical theory and must know the rudiments of medicine as it relates to public health.*

- *He must understand the basics of the law and know the legal precedents for various measures concerning drainage rights and lighting, and he must be able to prepare a contract which is clear and unambiguous and will not rise to litigation later.*

- *Finally, since town sites and encampments are to be oriented without a magnetic compass, he must have enough of a basic knowledge of astronomy to work out the directions from the sun and stars, and cali-*

brate sundials at different latitudes (De Camp 1963, 27).

Not only did these ancient people develop building techniques, they also came up with codes that insured public safety. Laws and other historical documents from Babylon, Greece, and the Roman Empire show that, even then, engineers had a responsibility for the safety of others.

- *If a builder build a house for a man and does not make its construction firm, and the house which he built collapse and cause the death of the owner of the house—that builder shall be put to death.*

- *If it causes the death of the son of the owner of the house—they should put to death the son of the builder.*

- *If it causes the death of a slave of the owner of the house—he shall give to the owner of the house a slave of equal value.*

- *If it destroys property, he shall restore whatever it destroyed, and because he did not make the house that he built firm and it collapsed, he shall rebuild the house that collapsed at his own expense.*

- *If a builder builds a house for a man and does not make its construction meet the requirements and a wall falls in, the builder shall strengthen the wall at his own expense (Miller 1966, 41).*

Because construction and maintenance of irrigation canals were vital for ancient Mesopotamia, its legal code included many rulings on this subject:

The gentleman who opens his wall for irrigation purposes, but did not make his dike strong enough and hence caused a flood and inundated a field adjoining his, shall give grain to the owner of the field on the basis of those adjoining (De Camp 1963, 46).

Hammurabi (1792-1750 B.C.) wrote the following to his governors about the repair of canals:
Unto Governor Sid-Iddinarn say: Thus saith Hammurabi. Thou shalt call

out the men who hold lands along banks of the Dananum Canal that they
may clear out Damanum-Canal. Within the present month shall they com-
plete the work . . . (De Camp 1963, 46).

Ancient history includes numerous accounts of catastrophic failure of buildings and other structures. In the Gospels, Jesus even mentions in passing the collapse of a tower in *Siloam* (Luke 13:4).

The Roman historian *Tacitus* (A.D. 55-120) describes the failure of an amphitheater grandstand. In another case, *Tacitus* describes a disastrous collapse of a structure that occurred in A.D. 27, which caused many casualties. According to his description, a builder by the name of *Atilius*, coming from the poorest part of the city, obtained a building permit to construct a temporary wood-framed amphitheater near the town of *Fidenae* in the valley of *Tiber*. At the first exhibition held in the amphitheater, shortly after the crowd had taken their seats, the entire structure collapsed, burying the spectators in debris.

The people of *Fidenae* were shocked by the accident, which according to the official investigation, accounted for 50,000 casualties, including those killed or injured. The town's noblemen provided their palaces as hospitals while aristocratic women served as nurses to the injured.

As in the present day, following a catastrophe of this type, the local government or Senate issued new building-code regulations for safety of public buildings used for assembly; and as punishment, the contractor *Atilius* was deported from Italy.

Instead of an actual building code, the early Greeks had a complex collection of requirements for the contractual relationship between builder and client. During a restoration project, work specifications were found inscribed on fragments of a building dating to 341 B.C. by Heinrich Latterman, who also found the names of both the contractor and the building inspector engraved on stone, as well as the date of completion.

A typical building specification for the construction of stone masonry walls described the manner in which the stones were fitted together, inspection by the architect, insertion of iron dowels into each stone, and the locking of the dowels with molten lead. The specifications also required that the building inspector should be present during the installation of the dowels and lead before the work was covered up.

These ancient specifications were very similar to the regulations of a present-day building code and the construction specifications prepared by contemporary architects and structural engineers.

Timeline

The following timeline shows many societies and historic events that contributed knowledge and skills:

9000-6000 B.C.
> Early farming communities

7000-6000
> Jarno, oldest known permanent settlements with crude homes, barley and wheat crops, and livestock including goats, sheep, and pigs
>
> Jericho's first walls erected

6000-5000

5000-4000
> Early Chaldeo-Assyria Empire (4000-1200 B.C.)

5000-3500
> Pre-Sumerians

4000-3000
> Semitic migration to Egypt and the Euphrates Valley (3500 B.C.)
>
> First long paved road in Mesopotamia (3500 B.C.)
>
> First wheeled vehicles (3000 B.C.)
>
> First cuneiform writing

3500-1900
> Walls of Babel built (1900 B.C.)

3000-2000
> Sumerian Empire (3000-2370 B.C.)
>
> First dynasty of Ur (2880-2400 B.C.)
>
> King Gilgamesh of Sumer (2700 B.C.)
>
> Semitic migration to Syria and Palestine (2500 B.C.)
>
> Sargon the Great (2334-2279)

2000-1900

Nimrod founds the Babylonian Empire (1989 B.C.)

Abraham leaves Ur (1926 B.C.)

Amorite dynasty adopts Babylon

1900-1800

1800-1700

King Hammurabi (1792-1750 B.C.) Schools for writing, astronomy, astrology, and cuneiform tablets

Semitic slaves in Egypt

1700-1600

Abraham moves to Haran (1682 B.C.)

Hittites conquer Babylonia

1600-1500

1500-1400

1400-1300

1300-1200

Assyrian Empire (1250-626 B.C.)

1200-1100

Nebuchadnezzar takes Babylon (1124-1103 B.C.)

Rameses III rules in Egypt (1195-1164 B.C.)

1100-1000

1000-900

King Solomon (974-937 B.C.)

First Temple built in Jerusalem (969-962 B.C.)

900-800

King Ashumasirpal and Shalmaneser in Battle of Qarqar (853 B.C.)

800-700

King Tiglathpileser III (745-727 B.C.)

700-600

Assyrians defeat Israel and Samaria (721 B.C.)

King Naboplasahr (625-605 B.C.)

King Nebuchadnezzar, son of Naboplasahr, rules (604-562 B.C.)

King Cyrus rules Persia (559-529 B.C.)

Jews return to the Holy Land

As seen above, the ancient engineer was a composite of many cultures, languages, skills, and governments. It began with the first clay brick building, irrigation channel, and measuring device, to blossom into the construction of the Holy Temple in Jerusalem.

Summary

The master builder of the ancient world was a combination of many of today's specialists. He was primarily an architect that laid out the project to function as a royal palace, like the Zuggurat, or House of Worship, similar to Jerusalem's Holy Temple. He was the structural engineer that designed the stone columns and masonry arches to resist gravity and earthquakes. He was the military engineer that built fortresses against potential enemies and the inventor of siege engines that destroyed fortress walls. He was the sanitary engineer designing distribution of clean water by aqueducts and collection and disposal of waste by sewers. He had an artist's soul, creating beautiful mosaic floors, and the hand of a sculptor that chiseled classic Ionic and Corinthian capitals. All of these and more were within the talents of the biblical master builder.

2

The Land

T HE LAND IS BOTH CANVAS AND PALETTE FOR THE ENGINEER. ON
 his canvas, he positions his creations—the palaces, temples, aqueducts, and harbors. From his palette, he withdraws his materials. To fully
understand the work of ancient engineers, we need to first look at the land
in which they lived.

Although we will cover advances in engineering from Mesopotamia
through Egypt to Rome, our consideration centers on the Middle East,
particularly the land of Israel. Not only has this little strip of earth proven
historically significant, it also offers a rich variety of geographical and
geological features. We will get a good idea of the engineer's struggle
with the land as we look at this region.

Many civilizations have left their mark on the Holy Land. It was known
as Canaan in Abraham's time; then Eretz Israel ("the Land of Israel") after
the Israelites conquered it. Following the death of King Solomon, a rebellion divided the land into Israel in the north (also known as Samaria, for
its capital, or Ephraim, for its largest tribe) and Judah in the south. Under

the Romans, the southern region was called Judea. They renamed the entire area Palestina, a derivation of Philistina, the name of the coastal region, where the Philistines had lived. Under Ottoman and British rule, the name changed to Palestine, and with the establishment of the Israeli state in this century, it became Eretz Israel again. During its lengthy history, this land has been occupied by Egyptians, Phoenicians, Israelites, Babylonians, Persians, Greeks, Romans, Arabs, Ottoman Turks, and western Europeans. All left their remembrances. Each new society has literally built on the foundations of the old one. Thus many structures uncovered by modern archaeologists are composites of various periods and cultures.

Fig. 1. Topographical view of ancient Israel

The Dead Sea and Jordan River follow the Great Rift Fault, one of the lowest-elevation regions on earth. The Judean hills *rise immediately to the west of the Dead Sea, creating a ridge that runs northward and then veers toward the coast. To the west of this ridge are rolling foothills and a coastal plain.*

Woodlands lay along the northern Mediterranean coast. Grasslands flourished eastward, toward the Sea of Galilee and in the foothills. The Dead Sea area and southward was very arid, growing only desert shrubs (Canaan 1954, 74; Carta 1977, 36; Reader's Digest Editors Atlas 1981, 39; Reader's Digest Editors People 1981, 315).

Fig. 2. Holy Land and surrounding areas

Babylonia was part of Mesopotamia and is generally described as the fertile area adjacent to the Euphrates and Tigris Rivers. Mesopotamia also included Sumer, Akkad, Nachariah, Assyria, Aram, Mittania, and Elam. This ancient land was first settled by the Sumerians in the third millennium BCE; then dominated by the Akkadians for 200 years. The Amorites then ruled northern Babylonia, but between 824-612 BCE, the Hittites and Assyrians took control of the land.

This Great Empire extended over the whole Fertile Crescent, the Negev and included the Egyptian Kingdom. After that, the Neo-Chaldeans under Nebuchadnezzar II ruled the country. But 25 years after his death, the Persians under King Cyrus took control of the land.

The geography of Mesopotamia consisted at the time of a crescent-shaped fertile valley along the Euphrates and Tigris Rivers. The former, known in the Bible as "The Great River," flowed from the mountains in Turkey through Syria into Iraq. East and generally parallel to the Euphrates, the Tigris flows from the mountain range in Turkey south to the northeastern tip of Syria, past Baghdad, and finally joins the Euphrates before discharging into the Persian Gulf. West of the fertile area was the Arabian Desert and east the Zagros Mountains. It is believed to have been the site of the Biblical Garden of Eden.

Fig. 3. Regions of the Holy Land

As this figure shows, there is a general similarity between the geography of the Holy Land and the State of California. Both have mountain ranges parallel to their coastline (the Judean Hills and the San Gabriel Mountains). Each has fertile valleys between the ranges (Galilee and the Sacramento Valleys), a great arid area beyond the mountains, (Judean and Mojave Desert), and a desolate desert surrounding lakes without fish (the Dead Sea and the Salton Sea).

Geography

Only 150 miles long and fifty-four miles across its greatest width, *Canaan* is about the size of New Jersey. Yet it sports a variety of topographical features and climatic conditions. Its 6,000 square miles include desert, farmland, and mountains.

The land is bounded by the Mediterranean Sea to the west, the Lebanon mountain ranges to the north, the Transjordan desert to the east, and the Gulf of Aqaba on the south. We can denote five major regions of the land itself:

- The *Galil*, or Galilee, rather mountainous (some peaks reach 3,000 feet)

- The valleys, including *Zevulun* (southeast of Haifa), *Jezreel*, Jordan, and *Beth-shean*

- The coastal plain, from Haifa south to *Migdal Gad.*

- The hill areas, including the hills from *Samaria* through Judea (where Jerusalem is located)

- The *Negev*, the triangle of desert in the south

An east-west cross section of the land (Fig. 4) shows the extreme topographic changes. The land rises from sea level, at the Mediterranean, to 2,500 feet above sea level, at Jerusalem, then plunges to 1,250 feet below sea level, at the Dead Sea.

Mountains parallel the coastline, providing a mild, subtropical climate for most of the land. To the east, the Jordan Valley is hot and arid, burned by the wind that sweeps from the Arabian deserts. But the coastal plain and foothills west of the mountain ridge enjoy moist air from the sea and regular rainfall.

The prevailing winds in the eastern Mediterranean create a natural division of the land into northern, central, and southern zones. The north has abundant rainfall, the center has moderate moisture, and the south is dry.

Intermittent rains generally begin in mid-October, peak in January, and end in the spring. This is when the crops grow. In the summer, the intense heat and air burn up the vegetation. The land also contains many important minerals. Copper, manganese, and barites are found near *Elath*, and the Dead Sea has iodine, bromine, calcium, and salt. Near the Lebanon border there are clay and basalt, and glass sand is mined at *Beersheva.* Galilee has *pozzolana,* Gezer has marble, and bituminous limestone is found near Haifa and Jerusalem. Other mineral resources include sulfur, gypsum, fire clay, kaolin, feldspar, and potash (Canaan 1954, 74; Reader's Digest Editors Atlas 1981, 38).

Jerusalem, one of the major cities we will consider, has a rich geological mixture: various types of colored limestone, much of which can be easily cut and used in building. Located on the ridge of the Judean mountains, Jerusalem is bounded on the east by the Judean desert. One ancient caravan route wound through that desert, from Jericho to Jerusalem and on to the Mediterranean. Another major route ran north-south along the Judean mountains. Thus Jerusalem lay at a crossroads. Yet its position on

Fig. 4. Cross section of the Holy Land

This cross section of Canaan, cutting across the land at the latitude of Jerusalem, shows both topographical and climatic features of the region. Winds from the Mediterranean Sea push moist air eastward, and the rising terrain pushes it up, where it turns to rain, which waters the western slopes of the Judean hills. Peaking at Jerusalem, the now-dry air descends into the Jordan Valley.

Beneath the fertile soil lies granite bedrock covered by limestone and chalk. East of the Jordan, Nubian sandstone sits atop the granite. The Great Rift Fault, in which the Jordan River and Dead Sea lie, is lined with sediment.

Fig. 5. Profile along the Jordan River

As this profile shows, most of the Jordan River is below sea level, as are the Sea of Galilee and the Dead Sea, the lowest spot on the earth. Only a few miles west of the Jordan River lays Jerusalem, which is 2500 feet above sea level, and Mount Hermon, which towers 12000 feet above sea level.

the mountains made the city easy to defend, and a nearby spring supplied its water needs.

This spring, the *Gihon*, still gurgles near the present village of *Silwan*, in the Kidron Valley. King Hezekiah built an impressive tunnel in 701 B.C. to lead the waters inside the walled area of the city, to the Pool of *Siloam* (2 Kings 20:20). Both Old and New Testaments mention Siloam (John 9:7; Nehemiah 3:15).

Most of the existing houses of Silwan are built of stone block, as they were in biblical times, with some recent concrete-block additions. As in ancient days, each flat, plastered roof collects the rain, funneling it to a pipe that leads to a water barrel or underground cistern. The houses cluster on both sides of the steep valley, among the ancient caves. A simple footpath winds between the dwellings. A narrow paved road traverses the bottom of the valley, leading toward the spring and reservoir.

Babylonia

Long before the founding of Israel, the ancient people living in Babylonia built a civilization on clay, first writing and pictographs, potter's wheels, an extensive water system, a water clock, and a powerful army. They invented engraving and inlay, and they built magnificent cities and buildings that included Ziggurats, the Tower of Babel, and the Hanging Gardens of Babylon.

It is said that the outer walls of the Hanging Gardens were ten miles long, encircling vaulted terraces built one above the other, each resting on cube-shaped pillars. Stairs were used for ascent to the terraces, each beautifully landscaped and irrigated by a type of chain pump that drew water from the adjacent Euphrates River. The arts and skills that went into Babylonia continued in one form or another over thousands of years to the Holy Land.

3

Ancient Dwelling Places

YOU CAN STILL SEE THE REMNANTS OF THE HISTORY OF HOUSING throughout the Mideast. Housing started with caves, such as those in the Silwan village of modern Jerusalem. Nomadic tents were the next step—such as those still used by Bedouins in the Negev and Jordanian deserts. Then our biblical ancestors developed homes of sun-dried and kiln-baked brick or simple stone-and-rubble huts such as those now found in Hebron and Acco (Morgan 1960, 38).

Tent Dwellings

The people of Israel must have enjoyed the nomadic life, since some remained in tents even after towns and villages sprang up.

Nomadic people needed light, portable shelter, made of readily available materials, so they made tents of wood poles and skins or cloth.

A framework of wooden poles cut from trees formed the basis of the tent. In the center of the structure, the tent dweller erected three poles, each about two meters long, which formed the peaked roof. Beside the poles, to either side, ran a parallel row of slightly shorter poles that formed the dwelling's walls.

Over this stretched a covering of camel skin, goatskin, or goat's-hair cloth, sewn together to the proper dimensions. Using leather thongs that formed loops in each corner, the tent dweller stretched the sewn covering over the poles until it created a taut building secured by wooden stakes. Neither the elements nor the impact of humans or animals could easily topple it.

At the doorway, folds of fabric protected the opening. The floor was merely beaten earth, often covered with woven rugs. A fabric curtain or reed screen would divide the tent's interior into two rooms. Visitors were welcome in the front section, but the owner reserved the back room for private and family life. A wealthy man might have separate tents for his wives, as did Abraham and Jacob (Genesis 24:67; 31:33).

Large tents were commonly used for public meetings. The Old Testament, for instance, gives specifications for the elaborate tabernacle used by the wandering Israelites for public worship (Exodus 26, 27, 36-40).

Houses of Clay Brick

Due to the lack of natural stone and timber in Babylonia, sun-dried clay bricks or blocks were the main material for construction. By the third millennium, true-fired bricks were used. When people forsook the nomadic life and settled down, they needed more durable homes. In settlements such as Jericho, the oldest known town in the world, builders made huts with walls of sun-dried clay bricks. Roofs consisted of wooden beams, branches, and grass. In later times, builders covered the roofs with clay, forming a surface strong enough to walk on and smooth enough to channel rainwater down into a waiting jar or cistern.

Before forming clay into bricks, the ancient builder added straw or other fibrous material to the mixture. This provided the tensile strength lacking in the clay itself and kept the bricks from cracking when dried. The Bible assumes the necessity of straw in brick making when it tells how the Egyptian taskmasters stopped supplying straw to the captive Israelites, but demanded the same quota and quality of bricks (Exodus

5:7-19). Making bricks without straw was apparently not an option; the Israelites had to gather their own straw and still produce just as many bricks (Morgan 1960, 42).

About two feet thick and seven or eight feet high, walls of sun-dried bricks provided rather good insulation, deflecting the direct heat of the sun but retaining some warmth for the cold nights. In later times, a coating of lime plaster made the walls relatively waterproof.

The roofs were held up not only by the clay walls, but also by wooden beams spaced throughout the house's perimeter. The bricks would be laid to provide supports for the ends of unfinished tree limbs, which were sometimes hewn into rectangular shapes. (See Fig. 7.)

The common people's homes usually consisted of one room adjoining a walled-in yard. The roof served a double purpose as a parlor and sleeping area. Some homes had granaries nearby; either in lined underground pits or above ground, in domed structures made of beaten earth.

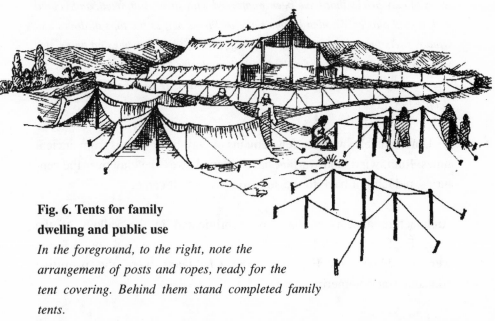

Fig. 6. Tents for family dwelling and public use

In the foreground, to the right, note the arrangement of posts and ropes, ready for the tent covering. Behind them stand completed family tents.

In the background is a representation of the Israelite tabernacle. Linen sheets stretched out on bronze posts and silver curtain rods encircle the courtyard. The main tent materials included woven fabric, goatskin, dyed ram's skin, and other light animal hides, supported by posts of acacia wood (Miller, 1978, 28, 29).

Fig. 7.
A typical
clay-brick house
The cutaway portions
in this drawing show the
details of the construction of clay-brick
houses. The foundation is made of uncut stones and rubble; the
walls of clay bricks that have been reinforced with straw, sun dried, and coated
with a mud plaster. Wooden beams serve as lintels across the tops of doors and
windows. Timber beams also form the roof. Covered by branches and twigs, this
would support a clay deck finished with lime plaster, sturdy enough to walk on.
The floor of the dwelling would be stamped earth (Reader's Digest Editors
People 1981, 140).

Unfortunately, we have few remains of clay-brick homes from ancient times. Rain, wind, and warfare have chipped away the clay over the centuries, reducing it back to the soil from whence it came.

Architecture appears to have been originated in the valleys of the Tigris/Euphrates and Nile Rivers, as the oldest existing monuments found were Chaldean and Egyptian. The Chaldeans were the primitive Akkadians and Sumerians.

Ur

Huge and intricate mazes of narrow unpaved streets six-to-eight feet wide ran behind the protective walls of the City of Ur. Clay brick windowless houses lined both sides of the streets. Most were two stories in height with a central patio.

Babylon was the oldest city in the world. Its poor people built circular mud-brick huts supported by a center post, with walls packed with reed and clay. The wealthier citizens constructed three-story houses with flat roofs buttressed with timbers packed with mud.

Stone Buildings

Since much of the land of Canaan was rich in limestone, this became a widely used building material. Even the common people found it fairly easy to gather uncut stone blocks and pile them up, forming walls. Sometimes they even coated them with a lime plaster. Wealthier homes used carefully cut and dressed stones.

Because of the weight of the stone walls, these homes needed strong foundations, wide enough to distribute the weight over the subsoil, so the building would not sink, and deep enough to keep water from seeping in during the rainy season. Thus builders dug trenches and laid large stones in them. Because the blocks were not uniform in size, the foundation trenches might be dug at different depths—whatever was necessary to make the tops of the stones level. Where especially wide foundations were needed, two rows of large stones would be laid along the outside edges of the footing, and the space between them would be filled with smaller stones (Paul 1973, 30-33).

In the palace at Tell al-Al, south of Ashkelon, along the Mediterranean coast, archaeologists have excavated a better-engineered foundation, dating back to 3200-3000 B.C. Quarried out of bedrock, a trench was lined with carefully cut stones. The upper half of these stones protruded above the floor line of the house, creating a curb at the base of the masonry walls.

The roofs of typical stone-block houses were the same as those of the clay-brick dwellings. Timber beams and branches supported a layer of clay, covered by lime plaster. On their roofs, some homeowners kept cylindrical limestone rollers to compact the clay after each rain (Paul 1973, 30, 31; Reader's Digest Editors People 1981, 98).

Fig. 8.
A typical
stone-block
dwelling
Without its roof, this house
is made of stone blocks. Note the
wooden posts inside the house and the door
lintels of stone. The wooden stairway leads to an open-
ing in the roof. As with clay-brick houses, the roof would be
made of wooden beams and branches, supporting a deck of plastered clay.

For the common people, roofing timbers were generally sycamores, although more expensive homes used cedar or cypress. If the building was too wide for a single timber to span, builders might install interior posts of stone or timber. These would support interior beams, which the shorter timbers could reach.

Roman engineer-architect *Vitruvius*, writing in the first century B.C., advised builders on the selection of wood and the construction of roof decks:

> *As soon as common oak boards get damp, they warp and cause cracks in the floors. But if there is no winter oak, and necessity drives, use common oak boards cut pretty thin; for the less thick they are, the more easily they can be held in place by being nailed on. . . . As for Turkey oak or beech or ash, none of them can last a great age.*

When the wooden planking is finished, cover it with fern, . . . [or]
straw, to protect the wood from . . . the lime.

Then, upon this lay the bedding, composed of stones not smaller than
can fill the hand. . . . Mix the broken stones in the proportions, if it is new,
of three parts to one of lime; if it is old material used again, five parts
may answer to two in the mixture. Next, lay the mixture of broken stone,
bring on your gangs, and beat it again and again with wooden beetles
into a solid mass, and let it be not less than three quarters of a foot in
thickness . . . (Morgan 1960, 202).

As in clay-brick homes, the roof was more than a covering for the house. It became an additional living area, often used for sleeping and dining. Women might use it to dry figs, dates, or flax in the hot sun. In the Book of Acts, the apostle Peter prayed on a roof in Joppa and saw a vision there (Acts 10:9-11). The roof was reached either by a stone staircase attached to an exterior wall or by ladder from the inside, which led up through a hatchway in the roof. For safety, a parapet generally surrounded the roof area.

Unlike clay-brick houses, many remains of stone buildings still exist in Israel, representing a broad range of architectural and decorative styles.

Floors, Doors, and Windows

Common people's homes usually had floors of stamped earth, though some added limestone chips to make it harder. The flooring in houses of the wealthy consisted of stone slabs, often finished with terrazzo, a mixture of cement and marble chips (Morgan 1960, 202). Vitruvius offered guidelines for flooring:

With concrete flooring . . . great pains and the utmost precaution must be
taken to ensure its durability. If . . . concrete flooring is to be laid level
with the ground, let the soil be tested to see whether it is everywhere solid,
and if it is, level it off and upon it lay broken stone with its bedding. But
if the floor is either wholly or partially filling, it should be rammed down
hard with great care (Morgan 1960, 202).

He adds specifications for indoor floors:

> *On this lay the nucleus, consisting of pounded tile mixed with lime in the*
> *proportions of three parts to one, and forming a layer not less than six*
> *digits thick. On top of the nucleus, the floor . . . should well and truly [be]*
> *laid by rule and level.*
>
> *After it is laid and set at the proper inclination, let it be rubbed down*
> *so that, if it consists of cut slips, the lozenges . . . may not stick up at dif-*
> *ferent levels . . . for the rubbing down will not be properly finished unless*
> *all edges are at the same level plane (Morgan 1960, 203).*

Fig. 9.

Construction of a

clay-brick dwelling

Builders are setting
wood posts and
beams atop newly
fashioned walls of
sun-dried bricks cov-
ered with limestone. On
top of the wooden framework,
they will place branches to form a deck of clay. Then they will cover it with lime
plaster, to waterproof the roof and increase its durability. The deck will be sloped
and curbed so that captured water can be diverted to a cistern.

Doors and windows often received elaborate treatment in wealthier homes. As the stone dwelling developed, architects began to pay more attention to the aesthetic appearance of the façade—balancing shapes, masses, detail, and shadows—and placing the windows and doors accordingly.

Windows were usually closed by shutters. In the Hellenistic period, builders tried a variety of translucent materials as windowpanes: oiled cloth, sheepskin, horn, mica, and gypsum shaved to thin sheets. These became obsolete as clear glass was introduced. Though glass making goes back to the early Egyptians, and the Phoenicians improved on it, not until Roman times did glass became clear enough to let light through (Paul 1973, 36, 37; De Camp 1963, 178).

Doorways usually consisted of a pair of doorposts anchored to a stone sill or threshold at the bottom and spanned by a wooden or stone lintel across the top. Sometimes the threshold was set a bit higher than the floor, to prevent dirt or water from entering.

A heavy wooden door pivoted on a shaped stone socket embedded in the sill. The door generally swung inward. To create wider doorframes, the builder could add a center post for support, and two half-doors would pivot at the outside posts and meet at the center. For security, a crossbeam bolted the doors on the inside and was anchored to the masonry wall. When set across the doors, this crossbeam would effectively lock them against intruders.

The size of the door varied. Doors were generally lower than a man's height in private dwellings, but much higher and wider in temples or palaces.

Fig. 10. Royal residence at Megiddo

This reconstruction, based on ruins found at Megiddo, shows some features of wealthier homes. The spacious palace is built of cut stone plastered with lime, on a foundation of uncut stone. It includes an interior courtyard and a large roof deck, where servants might have dried flax and milled grain. The stone stairway leads to an observation tower with a stone lintel across the ramparts (Canaan, 1954, 5)

4

Public Buildings

WE KNOW MORE ABOUT ANCIENT PALACES AND TEMPLES THAN we do about the homes of the common people. Because these structures were made of durable stone, they have remained, whereas the clay and wood of common dwellings have eroded. Therefore, most existing ruins are public buildings or royal residences—at least exposing their foundations and lower portions of walls.

Engineers of ancient times also paid a great deal of attention to the tombs of royalty. In some cultures, tombs resembled small palaces, with arcades and porticos, vaulted and domed ceilings, and ornate columns at the entrances, spanned by intricate friezes. While those entombed passed away centuries ago, many of these sturdy structures have stood the test of time, giving us important glimpses into the past.

Babylon is one of the oldest cities in the world. Since columns and posts were not yet developed or used, most public buildings were massive pyramidal or stepped structures. There is a great similarity between the temples of the Mayans and Aztecs in Mexico and Guatemala and those of

27

ancient Babylonia. The buildings in Mesopotamia fell into two categories: temples and palaces, each representing the two major institutions of their society.

Temples, the first monumental buildings, were not only religious centers but were also administrative and economic centers. These latter functions were later housed in the palaces.

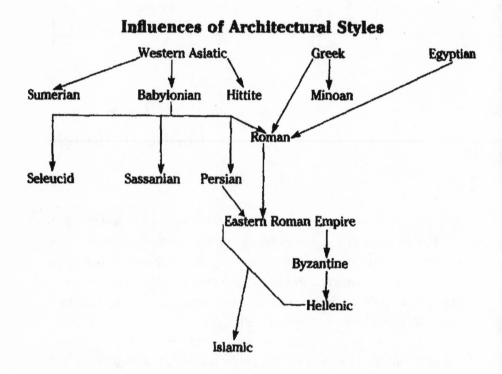

Influences of Architectural Styles

Fig. 11. Influences of architectural styles

The Hebrews were influenced by many different cultures: Egyptian, Phoenician, Babylonian, Persian, Greek, and Roman. We see the merging styles in the tombs of Absalom and Zechariah, which display the Egyptian cavetto cornice and pyramidal roof, but Doric and Ionic engaged orders (Hamlin 1904, 35).

Development of Architectural Design

Ancient civilizations were not isolated. Caravans crossed the desert, and merchant ships sailed the Mediterranean, Red Sea, Persian Gulf, and Arabian Sea, carrying not only goods, but knowledge, art, and ideas. Different civilizations throughout the ancient world developed their individual architectural styles, but they also borrowed from one another.

Three distinct architectural styles emerged in the *Bronze Age*: Western Asiatic, *Minoan*, and Egyptian.

Out of the Western Asiatic design came the *Sumerian*, Babylonian, and *Hittite* architectures, which in turn influenced the style of the Persians, *Seleucids,* and *Sassanians.*

Minoan architecture was developed from the Greek style, as were Roman techniques, which also incorporated *Sumerian*, Babylonian, *Hittite*, and Egyptian forms.

From Roman and Persian styles came the designs of the Eastern Roman Empire, Byzantine, and Hellenic cultures. All these combined to form the Islamic style (Allsopp 1965, 9).

Columns

According to *Vitruvius*, the *Doric* column (Figure 12) was based on the proportions of the human male figure. The average height of a Doric column is seven times its thickness. The column tapers as it rises, and its fluted shaft contains sixteen to twenty carved channels.

Typically the shaft was composed of several shorter stone cylinders, or drums, placed one on top of another. Each piece had to be light enough for two to four workers to carry and place. The three-part structure above the capital, or top of the column, is known as the *entablature,* and this is divided into the *architrave* (just above the column), the *frieze* or horizontal *cornice* (the next level, which might include carved words, pictures, or decorative designs), and the *typanum* or *pediment* (the upper sloping portion, which includes a raked cornice molding) (Landels 1978, 9).

The *Ionic* column (see Figures 13 and 14), *Vitruvius* said, was based on the female figure. By extending the height to about eight times the thickness of the column, its designers produced a more slender appearance. Also, the capital *volutes*, scrolling at the top of the column, suggest a woman's hair; the fluted shaft resembles the folds of a woman's garment; and the base of the column might represent the twisted cord of her sandals. Note also the entablature in this example: the three flat bands of the *architrave* and the ornamentation of *eggs-and-darts* and *dentils* at the top (Hamlin 1904, 48; Miller 1966, 51).

Some early columns were designed to represent trees and plants. This may have reflected the early use of timber to support buildings, as stone was worked to copy the material it replaced. The Egyptian *date-palm* column (Figure 16) mimics the palm trunk or bundles of reeds or saplings lashed together. The capitals had appropriate foliage carved in stone. The Egyptian *lotus column* (Figure 17) and clustered lotus column (Figure 18) also mirrored the plant world. The Greeks did the same thing with their *Corinthian* column (Figure 19), employing carved acanthus leaves in the capital (Hamlin 1904, 48).

Fig. 12. A Greek Doric column

Fig. 13. Front view of a Greek Ionic column

Fig. 14. Side view of a Greek Ionic column

Fig. 15. Detail of the Ionic scroll

Fig. 16. An Egyptian date-palm column

Fig. 17. An Egyptian lotus column

Fig. 18. An Egyptian column with clustered lotus

**Fig. 19. A Greek
Corinthian column**

Fig. 20. Shaping an Ionic capital
*The cushion-shaped capital of the Ionic column represented a woman's hair. The
shaft, which was usually fluted, represented the folds in her gown.*

Fig. 21. Entasis of columns

According to Vitruvius, the Roman design of columns basically followed that of the Greek. The unit of measurement was the diameter of the lower part of the column's shaft. The shaft contracted about one-sixth in diameter toward the capital under which it terminated by an astragal, or collar of small molding. At the base, it ended in a slight flare and fillet called the cincture. The entablature was about one-quarter the height of the whole column. The tapering proportions were developed to appeal to the viewer's eye and to add grace to the building.

Masonry Arches

The introduction of masonry arches was a major breakthrough in architecture, particularly in the design of public buildings. Previously, the size of the entrance to a room had been limited by the effective span of wood beams. But masonry arches could support much larger entrances, and by using them for interior design, builders could design much larger rooms.

The engineering involved is fairly simple. An arch consists of a series of shaped stone blocks that gradually span an opening by transferring their weight laterally to the adjacent blocks and eventually to the supporting abutments or walls. The arch essentially creates a beam that has been curved in the plane of the loads. Therefore, any section in an arch may be subjected to the same bending and shear stresses as an ordinary beam. In addition, the arch is subject to thrust from the components of vertical loads in the direction of the axis of the arch. In simpler terms, each block leans on the block beneath it and, in a way, presses on the block above it.

To ensure pure arch action, a masonry arch must meet three conditions:

1. The length of the span, or distance between supports, must remain constant.

2. The elevation of the ends must remain unchanged.

3. The inclination of the skewbacks (the first stones on the support, which begin the angle of the arch) must be fixed.

If any of these conditions are violated by settlement, sliding, or rotation of the abutment, the arch may fail.

It is apparent that the engineers and stonemasons of biblical times knew these rules as they built their arches. Just like modern engineers, they probably used the *line-of-thrust* or graphic analysis method to calculate the arch's dimensions. In fact, the criteria for arch design have changed little from ancient times to the present day (Hamlin 1904, 47-51).

Building with Arches

Fig. 22. A stepped corbeled arch
This probably represents the earliest form of a masonry arch.

Fig. 23. A straight stone arch
This stone post-and-lintel arch at Mycenae is known as the Lion Gate. It consists of dressed, uncoursed masonry and stone jambs (or posts) at each side of the opening. The posts support a stone lintel, carved into a single column, and two rampant lions (Harnlin 1904, 44).

Fig. 24. A square arch

The columns of the Citadel Gate, built at Hazor during King Ahab's reign, display carved proto-Aeolic capitals and represent construction during the days of monarchy in Jerusalem (Reader's Digest Editors Atlas 1981, 120).

Fig. 25. A simple round arch

Fig. 26. An elliptical stone arch

The main forces of an arch consist of the three radius points, the horizontal spring line, major and minor axes, and rise (the distance from the spring line to the crown). Units of cut stone include the skewback, which is at the spring line, the extrados, which forms the arch, and the keystone at the crown (Hamlin 1904, 81).

Fig. 27. A pointed stone arch

Later known as the Gothic arch, this type contains two radius points, which are at the spring line, with arcs that meet at the crown. By the eighteenth century, the wedge-shaped stones were voussoirs (Canaan 1954, 63).

Fig. 28. A Roman barrel vault

This structure was formed of semicircular arches and used in the construction of large rooms, culverts, aqueducts, and bridges (Hamlin 1904, 81).

Fig. 29. A groined vault

This complex structure was called a four-part vault or cross vault. Examples of this type of construction have been found adjacent to the Western Wall at the Temple Mount in Jerusalem. Key elements of this structure are the spring line, haunch, crown, and keystone (Hamlin 1904, 81).

Nebuchadnezzar's Palace

The city of Babylon built by *King Nebuchadnezzar* has been called the most magnificent of the ancient world, yet it lasted only a short time. After the king died in 562 B.C., his heirs failed to preserve his empire.

Nebuchadnezzar's Palace, one of the glories of that great city, lies in ruins today. Still, those ruins give us a glimpse of its majesty. The foundational platform of the palace was 700 yards long, 600 yards wide, and 70 feet high. This raised mound provided safety for the inhabitants. Entry was only through the guarded gates. This height also had some health benefits—palace residents could enjoy the prevailing breeze and freedom from insects.

The walls, piers, and buttresses were made with pale yellow bricks, set in fine cement. Resembling modern firebricks, these high-quality Babylonian building blocks were a foot square and three or four inches thick. Each was stamped with the name Nebuchadnezzar.

The Hanging Gardens of Babylon

The ancient Greeks beautifully described the Hanging Gardens of Babylon as follows:

"The approach to the Garden sloped like a hillside and the several parts of the structure rose from one another tier on tier . . . On all this, the earth had been piled . . . and was thickly planted with trees of every kind that, by their great size and other charm, gave pleasure to the beholder . . . The water machines [raised] the water in great abundance from the river, although no one outside could see it." (Diodorus Siculus)

"The Garden is quadrangular, and each side is four plethra long. It consists of arched vaults, which are located on checkered cube-like foundations. The ascent of the uppermost terrace-roofs is made by a stairway . . . "

"The Hanging Gardens has plants cultivated above ground level, and the roots of the trees are embedded in an upper terrace rather than in the earth. The whole mass is supported on stone columns . . . Streams of water emerging from elevated source flow down sloping channels . . . The waters irrigate the whole garden saturating the roots of plants and keeping the whole area moist. Hence the grass is permanently green and the leaves of the trees grow firmly attached to supply branches. This is a work of art of royal luxury and its most striking feature is that the labor of cultivation is suspended above the heads of the spectators . . . " (Strabo and Philo of Byzantium)

The structure is on the east bank of the River Euphrates about 50-km south of Baghdad. Built by Nebuchadnezzar, it was about 400 feet square and 80 feet high, (Diotorus Siculus)

The building was constructed by Hammurabi's son, Nebuchadnezzar II (604-562 B.C.) in honor of his wife. Legend has it that Nebuchadnezzar's wife was homesick for the mountainous land of *Media*. Babylon, built on the flat river plain, seemed too dull. So the king tried to build her an artificial, tree-capped mountain by the banks of the Euphrates. The result: another wonder of the ancient world, the famed *Hanging Gardens of Babylon*.

About 400 feet square and 75 feet high, the garden structure consisted of many parallel tiers of open arches. This allowed a solid platform to be built over each tier. A great mass of earth covered the topmost tier, and flowers, shrubs, and trees were planted there.

The structure was built mainly of bricks, since natural stone was hard to find in Babylon. The bricks were composed of clay mixed with chopped straw and baked in the sun. The bricks were then joined with bitumen, a slimy substance that acted as a mortar.

While rain was rare in Mesopotamia, the bricks would dissolve if wet. But the gardens had to be watered. Using an arrangement similar to the *Archimedes' screw,* engineers managed to provide an irrigation system for the gardens. To prevent water damage to the brick masonry, between the brickwork and the earth, builders installed a layer of reeds mixed with bitumen, and then a double layer of burned brick cemented with gypsum, and finally a coating of sheet lead. Upon all of this they placed a deep layer of soil for all types of trees and plants.

Tombs

THE GREAT PYRAMID

Built about 2600 B.C., *Cheops's* pyramid at *Gizeh* (Figure 25) is still the largest cut-stone structure in the world. Covering an area of thirteen acres (about eight football fields), it rises as high as a forty-story skyscraper. Its square base measures 755 feet wide.

Napoleon reportedly commented that there were enough blocks in the pyramid to build a ten-foot wall around France. The massive structure consists of 2.25 million stone blocks, averaging more than two tons apiece (Rossnagel 1964, 1-3); most of these are coarse desert *sandstone*

Fig. 30. The Great Pyramid of Gizeh

*Pyramid building took place between 3000 and 2000 B.C. The Great Pyramid of
the Gizeh group, near Cairo, measured 755 feet at the base and 482 feet high; it
required 2.25 million blocks of stone, with an average weight of two tons each.
The project required 100,000 workmen and took twenty years to build (Rossnagel
1961, 1).*

quarried locally. The casing of the pyramid, however, consists of closely
fitted limestone, quarried at Tura, about thirty miles south of Gizeh. Some
blocks are as heavy as fifteen tons. One interior burial chamber contains
nine blocks of granite, each weighing about 400 tons. These were quarried at Aswan, about 300 miles upstream on the Nile.

The pyramid was built for *King Khufu* (*Cheops* in Greek), of Egypt's
Fourth Dynasty. The methods of its construction remain a mystery. How
were those huge blocks transported and positioned? Horse-and-cart
machinery did not appear in Egypt for another eight centuries.

According to the Greek historian *Herodotus,* Khufu used forced labor,
conscripting 4,000 men at a time to work three-month shifts. They hauled
the stones from the quarry and put them in place. It took forty men to
move each block, *Herodotus* said, and the whole project took twenty
years. He also speculated about the machinery required for the project:

> *The pyramid was built in steps, battlement-wise, as it is called, or accord-
> ing to others, altar-wise. After laying stones for the base, they raised the*

remaining stones to their places by means of machines formed of short
wooden planks. The first machine raised them from the ground to the top
of the first step. On this there was another machine, which received the
stone upon its arrival, and conveyed it to the second step, whence a third
machine advanced it still higher (Miller 1966, 32-39).

But others have suggested that ramps of earth were used to pull the blocks
into position on the upper levels of the pyramid. One Egyptian picture from
about 2000 B.C. shows 172 men pulling a sixty-ton statue on a sled without
rollers. In this case, milk or some other fatty liquid might have been poured
on the ground to lubricate it. The most common theory holds that the pyramid workers pulled the stones on rollers that were set upon wooden rails.

The pyramid shows remarkable precision in surveying. One side of the
base lies within 0.1 degree of a true east-west axis. The other sides were
measured with such accuracy that there is only a 7.9-inch error in closure
of a true square. Each of the 206 courses of stone is set almost perfectly
level—the southeast corner is only a half-inch higher than the northwest
corner. The builders probably used channels of water to maintain a true
horizontal plane.

On the north side of the pyramid, fifty-six feet above ground, a small
entrance opens to a low, narrow tunnel, 150 feet long. This leads slightly
downward to the grand gallery, a hall twenty-six feet high. Adjoining this hall,
at the center of the pyramid is the main burial chamber, seventeen feet by 234
feet, with a ceiling nineteen feet high. The structure contains two other burial
chambers, one underground (in case the king died before the pyramid was finished), and the third (for the queen) placed between the other two. Tunnels that
branch off from the main tunnel reach these. (Rossnagel 1964, 1-4):

Whatever building method was used, it is obvious that the construction of this pyramid required four elements:

1. Precise use of simple devices

2. Unlimited manpower

3. Ability to organize and command that manpower, and

4. Unlimited time to complete the project

TOMBS OF ABSALOM AND ZECHARIAH

In the Kidron Valley, south of Jerusalem's Temple Mount, the Pillar of Absalom (the Tomb of Jehoshaphat) consists of a circular pyramid rising from a cylinder-shaped base. This rests on a square platform with a wreathed frieze that appears to be tied around it like a rope. A cylindrical pyramid forms the top of the tomb.

Fig. 31. The Tomb of Absalom

Sometime in the first century before Christ, this monument, called the Pillar of Absalom *or the* Tomb of Jehoshaphat, *was built east of Jerusalem, in a* necropolis *in the Kidron Valley. Although tradition says it is the burial place of King David's son* Absalom, *this building is not from that era (Canaan 1954, 18, 19).*

Adjacent to it is a second tomb, the *Tomb of Zechariah,* which betrays a mixture of foreign influences. Greek architecture shows in the *Ionic* columns, cut from reddish granite, which decorates the front. On top of the tomb is an Egyptian-style pyramid roof, with an Egyptian groove, or cavetto. The cube-like structure carved out of a rock, stands on a stepped base, which encloses the tomb area.

Though tradition associates these tombs with *Absalom* and the prophet *Zechariah,* the architectural styles place their construction later: the second or third century B.C. for Absalom's tomb and possibly as late as the first century A.D. for Zechariah's (Canaan 1954, 18, 19).

Fig. 32. The Tomb of Zechariah
Hewn from the side of a rock, this tomb includes an Egyptian-style pyramid above a square tower decorated with Ionic columns (Canaan 1954, 18, 19).

THE HERODIUM

Herod the Great built the Herodium as his burial place. It is the most impressive of many hilltop fortresses in Palestine. The existing hill was heightened and the fortress built at the summit, with four round lookout towers and three concentric walls. As with other hilltop citadels in Palestine, the *Herodium* is within signaling distance of one other citadel, so that reinforcements could be summoned in case of invasion (Netzer 1988, 18-33).

Building Laws

Property rights were as important in biblical times as they are now. Protection of surveyor's property monuments was noted in the following verses:

"You shall not remove your neighbor's landmark." (Deut 14:19)

"Cursed be he who removes his neighbor's landmark."
(Deuteronomy 27:17)

The Stone of Bohan, was a monument which showed the boundary between Judah and Benjamin (Josh 15:6).

ANCIENT BUILDING LAWS

King Hammurabi of Babylon (2297-2254 B.C.) enacted laws enforcing safe construction and had these laws inscribed on a six-foot high stone pillar.

In ancient Mesopotamia, construction and maintenance of irrigation canals were vital. Some of the laws on this subject were as follows:

"The gentleman who opens his wall for irrigation purposes, but did not make his dike strong enough and hence caused a flood and inundated a field adjoining his, shall give grain to the owner of the field on the basis of those adjoining" (De Camp).

A letter Hammurabi wrote to his governors about the repair of canals illustrated an example of the importance of maintenance:

"Unto Governor Sid-Iddinam say: Thus saith Hammurabi. Thou shalt call out the men who hold lands along banks of the Damanum-Canal that they may clear out Damamum-Canal. Within the present month shall they complete the work . . . " (De Camp).

There were many catastrophic failures of buildings and structures described by ancient writers. For example, in *Ancient Rome* by Rodolfo Lanciani, *Tacitus*, the Roman historian of 55 to 120 B.C., described the failure of a grandstand:

"Tacitus related that in the year 27 after Christ, a certain Atilius, a man sprung from the lowest classes of the city, obtained the right to build a temporary wooden amphitheater near Fidenae. An enormous crowd met at Fidenae, to enjoy the novelty of the exhibition, and at the same time to enjoy an excursion upon the green valley of the Tiber. These spectators had scarcely taken their seats on the wooden steps when, in a moment, and with a terrific crash, the whole structure gave way, and buried under

its ruins the entire assembly. Tacitus, who had at his disposal and who consulted the official reports of the police, assures us that the number of dead and wounded amounted to 50,000. The town was struck with profound terror and amazement. Noblemen turned their palaces into hospitals. Matrons and maidens of aristocracy took the office of nurses. The Senate made new regulations for the safety of public places of entertainment. Atilius, the author of the Fidenae slaughter, was only banished from Rome and Italy."

The early Greeks had complicated sets of specifications governing the contractual relationship rather than an actual building code. According to Heinrich Lattermann, in his restoration of building fragments built in 341 B.C., the completion date and the names of contractor and the inspector of construction were engraved on stone. Qualities of workmanship and the methods of inspection of a masonry project were described as follows:

"'He shall set the joints against each other, fitting, and before inserting dowels he shall show the architect all the stones (to be) fitting, and shall set them straight and sound and dowel them with iron dowels, two dowels to each stone of each course, and one to the stone at the corner.'

"It would seem that these stones were to be laid with their long sides touching. The corner stone of each course could then be doweled only on its short side, and could receive only one dowel comfortably.

"The clause is a natural one, and has good parallel in the Lebadeia inscription: 'He shall (perform) in person, in presence of the commissioners, the insertion of dowels and clamps and the pouring of lead, and shall close no (joint) without having shown it.'"

According to an archaeologist who examined the tablets, the inscription meant:

" . . . having made the margins of the joints as the architect shall order; 'and before leading the stones he shall show the architect the top surfaces

and all the joints, and shall dowel with iron dowels . . . ' This is the only procedure which will ensure accurate supervision of the preparation of contact surfaces."

The Bible contained building regulations to prevent people from falling off roofs. The typical roof was flat, and during the hot summer months, residents would have slept on the breezy rooftops. Deuteronomy 22:8 (RSV) stated:

When you build a new house, you shall make a parapet for your roof, that you may not bring the guilt of blood upon your house, if any one fall from it.

The Bible mandated roof-edge protection because the ancient Hebrews used rooftops for sleeping, preparing food, and doing other household chores. This regulation carried over to the modern building and safety codes.

5

Places of Worship

M OST NATIONS OF THE ANCIENT WORLD PRACTICED POLYTHEISM. Israel, with its devotion to its one true God, was a notable exception. The others worshiped numerous gods, associating them with various elements of creation—the sky, the earth, the crops, the sea, and others. When a nation conquered another, it often attempted to impose its gods on the weaker nation. The Book of Daniel, for instance, portrays the Babylonians forcing the captive Jews to bow before an image of gold (Daniel 3).

Such forced conversion, as well as subtler syncretism, created great similarities in how ancient culture worshiped their deities. Just as societies shared architectural ideas, they also shared ideas about gods. We see both of these facts in the remains of ancient worship places.

Polytheistic Places of Worship

Ziggurats

The early Babylonians built ziggurats to reach their gods. Ziggurat means "mountaintop," and it refers to the temple towers built on separate terraces near the temples. These were probably used as observatories—for the Babylonians were early experts in astrology. From these vantage points, priests could watch the moon and stars and chart their positions.

Many cities in Mesopotamia had ziggurats, but the best remaining one is at Ur. This seventy-foot-high structure measures 200 feet by 150 feet at its base and has three receding terraces. Each brick terrace was covered with soil and planted with trees and shrubs. The bottom terrace was black, the next red. At the top sat a shrine of enameled blue bricks. Side stairs led to a shrine on the lower level, a central stairway to the shrine at the top. This Ziggurat was for worship of the moon god and was built at the beginning of the Patriarchal Age of the Bible, before 2000-1500 B.C.

The Tower of Babel, mentioned in the Bible (Genesis 2:1-9), was probably the famous ziggurat at Babylon, built to honor *Marduk*, the head of the Babylonian pantheon. After several destructions and rebuilding efforts, Nebuchadnezzar II finally completed the structure about 600 B.C. It stood 300 feet high covered with colorful enamel bricks. Initially they were set in an enclosure, elaborately decorated, and built on an elevated platform. In the third millennium, the temple on a platform developed into a staged temple tower, or *ziggurat*.

Nebuchadnezzar's palace was built around five courtyards, which included his private quarters and harem. Two rooms behind the throne room contained oblong wells with a rectangular shaft between for maintenance access. A wheel and endless chain fitted with pottery buckets went down one well and up the other.

Temple of Bel

We see more Babylonian engineering skill in the Temple of Bel. This eight-story brick structure resembled a pyramid, with each story a bit smaller than the one below. According to Herodotus, the top floor contained a beautiful adorned temple. Worshipers climbed to the top on outside stairs, and seats were placed partway up, to allow rest from climbing.

The temple's structural design was rather simple. All walls were vertical, except for the third story, which had a slight backward tilt, but buttresses reinforced these walls. This gives further evidence that the ancient Babylonians had a good knowledge of design principles.

Fig. 33. Babylonian ziggurat

The ziggurat was the centerpiece of most Mesopotamian cities, built entirely of sundried brick reinforced with layers of reed matting (Reader's Digest Editors People 1981, 235).

Babylon had numerous chapels, shrines, and temples. It would not be unusual for a Babylonian city to contain fifty temples, fifty shrines to Marduk, and hundreds more shrines to earth gods. Some cities even "zoned" these buildings into a separate walled section known as "the sacred place."

The Babylonians liked height. Enamored with the gods of the heavens, the Babylonians built soaring temples. But they also created an illusion of height with recessed walls and platforms of solid brick. These platforms also protected the temples from flood damage.

Philistine Temples

Except for their struggles with the Israelites, recorded at length in the Bible, the Philistines left little mark on history. These ancient warriors inhabited five cities of the Canaanite plains, including the area known as Gaza. In this area, a recent excavation has uncovered an eleventh-century temple, the Temple of Beth-shean. Here the Philistines probably worshipped their fertility god, Dagon. The exterior walls were of masonry, but the interior had two rows of wooden columns that supported the roof. The Bible describes the mighty man Samson pushing apart two pillars in a Philistine temple and literally bringing down the house (Judges 16:23-

30). If the design of that temple was similar to this one, we can see how that might have happened.

Greek Temples

Many Greek temples remain from ancient times. The earliest of these were built as "god houses," dedicated to one god alone. In some cases, only priests were allowed to enter. In some of the major temples, Greek architects avoided the use of mortar by trimming the stone blocks to precise surfaces and using iron clamps anchored in notches by molten lead.

Jewish Places of Worship

The Jews differed from their neighboring nations. They worshiped not a collection of gods, but a single God, and their God defied physical representation. What did God look like? Not a bull, or a fish, or a frog, as other religions might suggest. Yahweh was not a sky god or an earth god or a sea god, but a God of all being. He had made humans in his image, but they were not to make images of him.

That stipulation came early in the Israelites' charter, the Ten Commandments:

> *"You shall not make for yourself a graven image, or any likeness of any-*
> *thing that is in heaven above, or that is in the earth beneath, or that is in*
> *the water under the earth; you shall not bow down to them or serve them*
> *(Exodus 20:4, 5 RSV).*

The God of the Israelites could not be simply cooped up in a building. He wrestled with Jacob by a stream (Genesis 32:22-30) and spoke to Moses from a desert bush (Exodus 3:1-6). As the Israelites wandered in the desert, their God was with them. Wherever they set up the tabernacle tent, it became God's holy place.

With the furnishings for the tabernacle, the Israelites began their crafting of sacred artifacts. Skilled artisans were employed to make the objects that would be used in Israel's worship. The law against graven images of

Fig. 34. Temple floor plans

Designs of temples varied and developed from place to place and through time. Here we see four recurring styles. The temple in antis plan (A) has a main hall and a porch whose roof is supported by two columns. The pro-style (B) has an open portico in front, with a colonnade of four columns supporting the portico roof. The amphiprostyle (C) has porticos in front and back, with rows of columns supporting the roof at both ends.

God remained in effect, but the artistry of the Hebrews could emerge in numerous worship symbols. Among those used by builders and craftsmen then and in the following centuries were palm trees (tree of life), *lullav* (palm branches), *ethrog* (citron fruit), acanthus leaves, birds, bulls, ram's horn, three crowns, the menorah or seven-branched candlestick (see figure 30), Jachin and Boaz (columns), the six-pointed star (the star of David), and signs of the zodiac.

The Ark of the Covenant was the most sacred of the Jews' objects associated with worship. This sacred chest, made along with other tabernacle furnishings, measured about forty-five inches long, twenty-seven inches wide, and twenty-seven inches high. It was overlaid with gold and had four gold rings around it, through which priests could insert poles of acacia wood to carry the Ark. The lid bore two cherubim of hammered gold, with their wings spanning the length of the chest. The Ark became the symbol of God's presence as the Israelites wandered from place to place. Inside it were placed the stone tablets of the Ten Commandments.

Solomon's Temple

When the Jews finally settled in their land, they needed a more permanent place of worship. A single Temple, centrally located, would call all Israel together from its far-flung settlements, to worship the true God. The great King David found the site, Jerusalem. His son Solomon, reigning over what proved to be the economic and military glory years of Israel, built the richly ornamented Temple.

Fig. 35. A carved Hebrew ornament
This design of the seven-branched lamp stand, candelabra or menorah, appears in various forms in early Hebrew buildings (Negev 1980, 104; Reader's Digest Editors Atlas 1981, 203).

This remains the greatest achievement of Jewish architecture. A variety of materials, many of them imported, were used, and Phoenician craftsmen were even brought in to assist on the project. From the biblical descriptions (1 Kings 6, 7; 2 Chronicles 3, 4), construction seems to have followed the Egyptian style, with successive courts, lofty entrance pylons, the sanctuary, and the Holy of Holies.

In its ornamentation, the Temple showed workmanship similar to the Phoenician and Assyrian styles, including cedar woodwork, decoration of hammered copper and gold sheets, and metal overlaying.

Built of limestone, the Temple towered fifty feet high and measured 180 feet in length and ninety feet in width. It stood on a sturdy stone platform, with huge retaining walls and impressive vaulted chambers. The main entrance faced east, flanked by two bronze pillars, named Jachin and Boaz. A vestibule led into a large main sanctuary. Banks of small windows, near the ceiling on the north and south walls, illuminated the sanctuary area.

It is said that no stone was visible from the interior of the Temple, since the ceiling was ornamented with sunken-wood panels and planks of cedar or cypress covered the floor.

"He lined the walls of the house on the inside with boards of cedar; from the floor of the house to the rafters of the ceiling, he covered them on the inside with wood; and he covered the floor of the house with boards of cypress" (1 Kings 6:15 RSV).

Note the other details of construction contained in the biblical account:

"He carved all the walls of the house round about with carved figures of cherubim and palm trees and open flowers . . ." (1 Kings 6:29 RSV).

"And he made for the house windows with recessed frames" (1 Kings 6:4 RSV).

" . . . And he made the ceiling of the house of beams and planks of cedar" (1 Kings 6:9 RSV).

"For the entrance of the inner sanctuary he made doors of olive- wood . . ." (1 Kings 6:31 RSV).

"In the inner sanctuary he made two cherubim of olivewood, each ten cubits high.... And he overlaid the cherubim with gold" (1 Kings 6:23, 28 RSV).

"For the cherubim spread out their wings over the place of the ark, so that the cherubim made a covering above the ark and its poles" (1 Kings 8:7 RSV).

The text also indicates that "neither hammer nor axe nor any tool of iron" was used in the Temple itself, indicating that the stone was precut in the quarry, to specification, and implying that the timbers were fitted with pegs (1 Kings 6:7 RSV).

Remarkably, the Temple was built in seven years, begun by King Solomon's orders in 967 B.C. and completed in 960 B.C. This First Temple stood for nearly four centuries, later destroyed by the armies of Babylonian King Nebuchadnezzar in 587-586 B.C. The Temple had three main sections (see figure 31): the unenclosed portico (*ulam*), just ten cubits deep and twenty cubits wide (a cubit is about a foot and a half); the sanctuary (*hekhat*), measuring forty cubits by twenty cubits; and the inner sanctuary (*debir*), also called the shrine or the Holy of Holies, twenty cubits by twenty cubits. The height of the vestibule and sanctuary was thirty cubits, but the Holy of Holies had a lower ceiling, forming a perfect twenty-cubit cube. Along both the side and rear walls extended a series of storerooms, two stories high. The exterior walls of the first-story rooms were thicker than those on the second story, to carry its extra weight (Fritz 1987, 38-49; Yaggy 1881, 440; Reader's Digest Editors Atlas 1981, 120; Reader's Digest Editors People 1981, 188).

The Second Temple

The people of Judea hated King Herod (40 B.C.-A.D. 4). He had allied himself to the conquering Romans, who became the power behind his throne. As if to prove his devotion to the Jews, Herod authorized massive building projects throughout the land—fortresses, harbors, and impressive Greek-style cities. His greatest project was the rebuilding of Solomon's Temple.

It had been over 500 years since the Babylonians had destroyed the First Temple, burning it and stealing sacred objects. Its glory was a distant memory. The Jews who returned from Babylonian captivity had rebuilt the Temple to a degree in 520-515 B.C., but this, too, had been ravaged and desecrated by conquering powers.

Although Roman engineers and designers were at his disposal, Herod enjoyed acting as his own architect. He based his vision for the Second Temple on Solomon's original, but the new Temple was much more grandiose, incorporating some Greek and Roman elements.

The Jewish historian Josephus details the construction of Herod's Temple, which began in 20 B.C. and was not completed until A.D. 62.

Ironically, the masterpiece of Herod and his heirs was enjoyed in its completed form for less than a decade. In A.D. 70, Roman armies quelled a Jewish rebellion and destroyed the Temple once again.

Herod's Temple was built on the same site as Solomon's, at the peak of rocky Mount Moriah. Tradition held that this was where Abraham had nearly sacrificed his son Isaac (Genesis 22:2; 2 Chronicles 3: 1). The peak was, of course, leveled off. Herod extended the original platform area, building retaining walls from large ashlar blocks. The resulting Temple Mount area formed a trapezoid about 910 feet wide in the south, 1,550 feet long on the east, and 1,575 feet long on the west—forty acres, or 172,000 square yards, in all. On the south side, a broad staircase of limestone led up to the Royal Portico and the Court of the Gentiles. The Temple and courtyards stood about 154 feet above the base of the Temple Mount. Within the mount itself were four or five levels of storerooms, stables, and cisterns.

Column walkways ran around the perimeter of the esplanade. The Royal Portico was the largest, according to Josephus, with 162 monolithic columns, each 4.6 feet in diameter and capped by ornate Corinthian capitals displaying rows of acanthus-leaf decorations. Three stories high, this portico included various halls often used by moneychangers and merchants who sold ritual objects.

The public would normally have entered from the southern staircase, through the Royal Portico and into the Court of the Gentiles, exchanging any foreign currency for silver shekels and then buying food, drink, or sacrificial animals.

The Court of the Gentiles surrounded the Temple and its interior courts, extending to the north and south. At the northwest corner of the Temple Mount sat the foreboding Antonia Fortress, housing the Roman soldiers assigned to Jerusalem.

The following is Josephus's description of the Temple Mount in Jerusalem:

"He also encompassed the entire temple with very large cloisters, contriving them to be in a due proportion thereto; and he laid out larger sums of money upon them than had been done before him, till it seemed that no one else had so greatly adorned the temple as he had done. There was a

large wall to both the cloisters; which wall was itself the most prodigious work that was ever heard of by man. The hill was a rocky ascent that declined by degrees towards the east parts of the city, until it came to an elevated level" (Josephus, Ant. Book XV Part 3).

This would have been a morose reminder to the Jews of their repression, but Herod might have found it strangely comforting.

Fig. 36. Plan of Solomon's Temple

On the eastern side of the interior Temple area, a gate (probably the Beautiful Gate, see Acts 3:2) led into the Court of Women. The Nicanor Gate led into the narrow Court of Israel, and then the Court of Priests, where the altar stood. Entrance to the Temple itself led visitors through a porch and into the sanctuary.

The roof of Herod's Temple was supported not by pillars but by wooden beams spanning the width of the building, a common element in Middle Eastern architecture of the time. The walls were built of neatly trimmed stones, with a beam of cedar was placed at every third course, strengthening the walls and providing support for the interior paneling (Hamlin 1904, 4).

Fig. 37. Plan of the Second Temple Mount in Jerusalem

In 18 B.C., Herod the Great extended the original limits of the Temple Mount to the north and south of where they had been at the time of Solomon's Temple. Major structures on the mount included the esplanade; the porticos along the perimeter; the Antonia Fortress, at the northwest corner; and the Temple area (Canaan 1975, 58, 59).

Fig. 38. Plan of the Temple Mount

Fig. 39. Temple Mount existing conditions at Herod's time

This shows the extent of the temple complex during King Solomon's time and the expansion by King Herod. Note the platform was extended to the north, west and south but not the east, which was at a steep slope of the mountain.

Fig. 40. Temple Mount section through the south end

When he rebuilt the Temple, Herod the Great constructed retaining walls of enormous ashlars up to thirty-six feet in length. They rest on the terrain's natural bedrock, which is fifty to sixty feet deep and provides excellent support for such a heavy structure. Between the bedrock and esplanade, builders supported the construction with backfill or created stone-arch storage rooms or reservoirs.

Fig. 41. Temple Mount section through Mount Moriah

To the left of the outcrop of Mount Moriah lies the filled-in Tyropoean Valley, to the west of the mount. Also shown are the Temple, the west and east porticos, and the Robinson Arch. Although the Bible fully describes the building and ornaments of Solomon's Temple and palace, it provides us with little information concerning the retaining walls and enclosure.

Fig. 42. Longitudinal section through the Temple

The rock outcrop that projects through the esplanade or platform is believed to have been the location where Abraham was ready to offer his son to God. Generally this is also regarded as the precise location of Solomon's Temple. Today the Dome of the Rock stands in its place. On the right, along the south wall, stands the Royal Portico. Bedrock, approximately 150 feet below the esplanade, forms the wall's foundation. The deck of the platform lies on man-made fill.

Fig. 43. Section through the Temple Mount

Figure shows the extent of the temple complex during King Solomon's time and the expansion by King Herod.

Fig. 44. Southern wall

The south elevation of the Temple Mount is the most impressive, rising high above the valleys below.

Fig. 45. East view of Temple Mount

This elevation shows the various phases of construction during different periods of time starting with the Solomon to the Herodian.

Fig. 46. Aerial view of Temple Mount
This three-dimensional reconstruction shows how the Temple Mount appeared when viewed from the southeast. The Royal Portico is the two-story structure in the foreground. The Temple complex faces the morning sunrise.

The limestone blocks had been quarried nearby, hauled on rollers, and hoisted by wooden cranes. Though most of the blocks measured about three feet wide and six feet long, some of the blocks for the retaining walls were up to thirty-five feet in length. One of Jesus' disciples remarked on the awesome beauty of the Temple:

" . . . *Look, Teacher! What massive stones! What magnificent buildings!"* (Mark 13:1 NIV).

The Temple Mount stood within the ancient city of Jerusalem, which was about 3.5 miles in circumference and had about 25,000 inhabitants. By the west retaining wall of the Temple Mount lay a ravine, crossed by masonry bridges and stairways. (Parts of these structures are now known as the Wilson Arch, the Warren Arch, and the Robinson Arch.) Further west was the Lower City. South of the Temple Mount were the old City of David (Ophel), the Kidron Valley, and parts of the Lower City. To the north lay the Upper City, with its theaters and wealthy homes. To the east loomed the Mount of Olives (La Perrousaz 1987, 36, 37).

Without plans for the Temple Mount that was built during Solomon's reign, archaeologists cannot know for certain where his workmen built the original retaining walls, but the present Temple Mount certainly covers more area than it did at the time of Solomon.

Various theories concerning the walls have been proposed. One holds that the present east wall dates back to the time of Solomon, because a continuous vertical joint exists about 107 feet north of the mount's southeast corner (Cornfeld 1981, 317).

Fig. 47. Present-day plan of the Temple Mount

Today the Dome of the Rock (Mosque of Omar), which stands directly over Mount Moriah, and the El Aqsa Mosque, on the south wall, dominate the Temple Mount. Arched rooms under the southeast esplanade form Solomon's Stables. A major reservoir and aqueduct lie nears the Dome of the Rock.

6

Ancient Building Materials

THOUSANDS OF YEARS AGO, BUILDERS USED ESSENTIALLY THE same materials as we use today. Without the aid of electric or gasoline-powered equipment, they had to manufacture and assemble the materials by hand. But just like modern contractors, they worked with stone, wood, and cement. The only significant modern structural material not available to them was prefabricated steel—yet they regularly used iron fittings to connect timber and masonry.

Geologists tell us the Holy Land was once at the bottom of a sea. The skeletons and shells of microscopic sea animals sank to the sea floor and were compressed, over the millennia, by the collecting sediment, forming white limestone. When the earth's own turbulence forced this sea floor up above sea level, it formed mountains of limestone and dolomite. As wind, water, and volcanic action eroded this material, it formed various kinds of soils and exposed rock.

These processes, in a way, stocked a "warehouse" full of materials for ancient builders. Solomon had limestone quarried for the Temple, but the ancients also used the soils—sand and clay. Other minerals and metals were mined and developed for use in construction—gypsum, pozzolana, iron, and other natural materials. Of course, trees were also cut and turned into usable lumber.

Builders dug sand from pits, washed it to remove dirt and salt, and then used it in mortar and plaster (beach sand was much too rounded to cohere well). With charcoal fires, they heated the ores of lime, gypsum, pozzolana, and metals, to convert them to construction material.

Clay made great bricks: just add water. Throughout the Mediterranean world, workers dug clay mud, added straw fibers to increase tensile strength, trampled it to the proper consistency, shaped it with wooden molds, and dried these bricks in the sun. Baked or fired brick, though long known, did not come into general use until the late Roman Republic. According to Vitruvius, sun-dried brick had been declared illegal for house walls in Rome, creating a need for kiln-fired clay bricks. Roman bricks came in many shapes and sizes, but the Romans seemed to prefer long, wide bricks that were only an inch and a half thick. These were less likely to warp or crack than thicker bricks.

Fig. 48. Brick making

This simple method of making bricks was common around 1500 B.C. in Egypt, Crete, and Asia Minor. Clay was mixed with water and straw, and the mixture was carried and poured into wooden molds, which were lifted, or removed, to allow bricks to dry in the sun.

Fig. 49. Brick molds

The man is making bricks with a mold. Some molds made one brick, others made two. They often had handles to facilitate lifting (Miller 1978, 33, 34).

Stone Masonry

Throughout the ancient world, builders used the various stone available to them. Construction materials included limestone, marble, sandstone, basalt, granite, and gneiss, among others.

Limestone was a nearly perfect material for construction in central Palestine. Plentiful in that area, it was soft and easy to quarry, but it hardened once exposed to the environment. To quarry the stone, masons drilled several holes into the rock in a straight line and drove wooden pegs into the holes. When soaked with water, these pegs expanded, exerting pressure on the stone and splitting it in a rather straight line. Using chisels and adzes, masons then shaped the rough faces of the stone. With square plumbs, levels, and measuring strings, they ensured straight planes and angles of the stone block, which would then be sanded with a loaf-like rubbing stone. Other stones were quarried in similar ways.

The stones used in any given locale depended on the geology of that area and the ability to quarry it. We have seen how the early Egyptians used sandstone for the bulk of the pyramids, because that was close at hand. The Babylonians, in the fertile plains of Mesopotamia, were more dependent on clay brick.

The Romans first used *tufa*, a soft tan and brown volcanic rock, in stone-masonry construction. Later they learned to use the harder *lapis gabinus* and *lapis albanas* (now called *sperona* and *peperino*), formed by the action of water on a mixture of volcanic ash, gravel, and sand. Still later, they used a hard, attractive limestone known as travertine (*lapis tiburtinus*). But unlike the volcanic rocks, it was not fire resistant; under heat, it crumbled into powder (Morgan 1960, 49).

**Fig. 50. Building
a masonry wall**

Fig. 51. Egyptian stonemasons dressing stone blocks

*Stonemasons cut and dressed blocks of stone in the quarry. The mason in the cen-
ter is drilling notches into the rock. On the left, another man drives wooden pegs
into such notches. When he soaks the pegs with water, they will expand, splitting
the rock. The mason at the right finishes a cut block's surface with a rubbing
stone (Miller 1978, 359-361).*

Fig. 52. Herodian smooth block

A smooth center panel projects about one ½-inch from the frame.

Fig. 53. Herodian rough block

Center panel projects about one ½-inch and is left rough to contrast with smooth borders.

Fig. 54. Quarrying

The stratified nature of the limestone in Jerusalem made quarrying easy. Driving wood pegs into a line of holes, then soaking the pegs with water, split the stone into blocks.

Fig. 55. A rubbing stone

This tool was commonly used to dress cut stone to a smooth surface.

Fig. 56. Building a masonry wall

Dressed stones were carefully placed, sometimes cemented with mortar, and masons plumbed the wall with simple, but effective, equipment.

Fig. 57. A stone wall consisting of header and stretcher blocks

Fig. 58. Wall construction
In a rubble stone wall, undressed, randomly shaped, un-coursed stones were set in naturally stable positions. This was also known as polygonal or cyclopean masonry.

Fig. 59. Types of finish joints in stone masonry

Fig. 60. Egyptian stonemasons dressing stone block

Fig. 61. A stone rubble masonry wall

Fig. 62. Plastering a masonry wall

A mason coats an ashlar or cut-stone masonry wall with lime plaster, using a wood pallet for mixing, a water jug for thinning, and a trowel for application and finishing.

Gypsum

As early as 3000 B.C., the Egyptians lined the inside of their pyramids with gypsum plaster. The Greeks also used a gypsum coating in their temples, and the Romans used it in their houses.

In Greek, the word *gypsos* means "plaster." A light-density, gray-white rock, gypsum can be ground to a powder, from which plaster of Paris is made. Chemically, the rock is known as dihydrous calcium sulfate ($CaSO_4 \cdot 2H_2O$). Heated in pits, gypsum gives up three-quarters of its water as vapor. As a result of this "calcining," gypsum can be easily crushed into a talc-like powder. When water is added again and it is mixed, it returns to its original rocklike hardness.

Mortar

The Israelites made mortar by mixing lime, sand, ashes, and water into a plaster. This was watertight enough to coat cisterns and reservoirs or for use as a finish coating for clay masonry walls and roof decks.

The Romans also used lime mortar between bricks and stone blocks on occasion. But in their public buildings, they generally relied upon iron clamps and the close fit of neatly trimmed stones to hold the structures together (Morgan 1960, 45).

Concrete

Near Vesuvius and elsewhere in Italy were deposits of a sandy volcanic ash. When added to lime mortar, this made cement that would harden even under water. They named this material *pulvis puteoli*, after Puteoli, an area that contained huge beds of the material. By mixing this cement with sand and gravel, the Romans created a sturdy concrete. But initially, the Romans apparently did not realize the possibilities of this new concrete, because they used it only in small amounts. Builders continued to apply mortars and plasters for centuries, until the new waterproof concrete began to catch on. Vitruvius described in detail the importance of the quality of sand used in mortar and concrete:

> *In walls of masonry the first question must be with regard to the sand, in order that it may be fit to mix into mortar and have no dirt in it. The kinds of pit sand are these: black, grey, red, and carbuncular. . . . The best . . . crackles when rubbed in the hand, while that which has much dirt in it will not be sharp enough. But if there are no sandpits from which it can be dug, then we must sift it out of riverbeds or from gravel or even from the sea beach. This kind, however, has these defects when used in masonry: it dries slowly . . . and such a wall cannot carry vaulting. . . . But pit sand used in masonry dries quickly, the stucco coating is permanent, and the walls will support vaulting. I am speaking of sand fresh from the sandpits. For if it lies unused too long after being taken out, it is disintegrated by exposure . . . and becomes earthy. . . . Fresh pit sand, however, in spite of all its excellence in concrete structures, is not equally useful in stucco, the richness of which, when the lime and straw are mixed with such sand, will cause it to crack as it dries on account of the great strength of the mixture. But river sand . . . becomes perfectly solid in stucco when thoroughly worked by means of polishing instruments (Morgan 1960, 44).*

Timber

Wood has been used in building since prehistoric times. Tree limbs and branches served as beams for the roofs and walls of many early homes.

The Bible indicates that parts of Palestine were rich in timber (1 Kings 10:27). The common people used sycamore, an inexpensive and readily available wood. The wealthy often imported cedar, fir, or *almug* from Lebanon or Syria. In public buildings, made mostly of stone, timber was generally used for the roof and doors.

Fig. 63. Dressing a log to a beam

Figure shows woodsmen shaping logs with adze, ax, and other tools.

**Fig. 64.
Dressing logs to
beams**
*Figure shows the phases of
shaping a round log to a rectangular
beam.*

King Solomon contracted with King Hiram of Tyre to import "Cedars
of Lebanon" for the Temple construction (1 Kings 5:6). Thirty thousand
Israelite lumberjacks were drafted and sent to Lebanon—ten thousand at
a time, in one-month shifts—to work with the local woodsmen in felling
trees for the Temple. The cedars and pines were then floated south in rafts
on the Mediterranean Sea. Israelite "carriers" apparently transported the
timber inland to Jerusalem.

In his Ten Books of architecture, Vitruvius offered numerous recom-
mendations for selecting and preparing timber:

> *Timbers should be felled between early Autumn and the time when
> Favonius begins to blow. For in spring all trees become pregnant, and they
> are employing their natural vigor in the production of leaves and of the
> fruits that return every year. In felling a tree we should cut into the trunk
> of it to the very heart, then leave it standing so that the sap may drain out
> drop by drop throughout the whole of it. In this way, useless liquid which
> is within will run through the sapwood instead of having to die in the mass*

of decay, thus spoiling the quality of the timber. Then and not till then, the
tree being drained dry and the sap no longer dripping, let it be felled and
it will be in the highest state of usefulness (Morgan 1960, 58).

Fig. 65. Timbers spliced with oak keys and yoke straps

Fig. 66. A lap-and-scarf butt joint
This is keyed together with hardwood and anchored with fishplates and bolts.

Fig. 67. A butt joint anchored with a key bolt and washer

Metals

You could almost date the birth of civilization to the discovery of metallurgy. Ancient cultures graduated at different times, in different ways,
from the Stone Age to the Bronze Age. The early chapters of the Bible
mention "Tubal-Cain, who forged all kinds of tools out of bronze and

iron" (Genesis 4:22 NIV). Ever since, people have used metals for tools and weapons.

As early as the third millennium B.C., the Egyptians opened copper mines on the Sinai Peninsula. The authorities sent their prisoners of war to work in these mines, digging with bare hands, hammers, wedges, bones, and horns. They used fire and vinegar for blasting.

Tin, which along with copper makes up the bronze alloy, was not plentiful in the Middle East, though sometimes it was smelted from richer ores (Ezekiel 22:18). Phoenician merchant ships brought tin and other metals to the Middle East from Tarshish—probably Spain (Ezekiel 27:12)

The earliest known use of bronze in the biblical region occurred in Sumer, in Mesopotamia, about 3000 B.C. The Sumerians had the ability to smelt copper and alloy it with small quantities of tin and arsenic. This process formed bronze, which was harder than copper yet could be cast in molds. Bronze became the dominant metal in the Middle East until iron superseded it in about 1200 B.C.

The Bible notes extensive use of bronze for Temple items:

> " . . . All these objects that Huram made for King Solomon for the temple
> of the Lord were of burnished bronze. The king had them cast in clay
> molds in the plain of the Jordan between Succoth and Zarethan. Solomon
> left all these things unweighed because there were so many . . ." (I Kings
> 7:45-47 mv).

Early Metal Molding

When ancient metalworkers realized that copper (and later bronze) melted at high temperatures, they learned to shape the metal by pouring it into molds of clay or stone. The first molds were simple depressions cut into stone or molded in clay, and the metal objects cast in such molds required much hammering and polishing.

Later metallurgists learned to use two opposing molds, avoiding much of the hammering and finishing work. Two-piece molds were crafted from stone or fired clay and held together by short dowels.

Through the second and third millennia B.C., bronze was widely used make farming tools, primitive stoves, and household items, such as cups, urns, and vases, as well as weaponry, including knives, spears, helmets, and shields.

Fuels

In addition to the more common uses of fire in the ancient world—cooking and heating—both furnaces for smelting and kilns for baking bricks required fuel.

Wood and charcoal were the most common fuels. For cooking, most preferred the slow-burning charcoal. Being almost pure carbon, it could reach extremely high temperatures, also making it ideal for smelting furnaces.

The best charcoal came from the hardest and closest-grained wood, such as oak and beech. Trees would be cut into small sections and partially burned in pits. These pieces would then be chopped into smaller pieces and bagged for shipment.

Iron

The Roman historian Pliny described iron as *"the most useful and the most fatal instrument in the hand of man."* Harder than bronze, it rapidly made other tools and weapons obsolete. The passage from bronze technology to iron technology had significant geopolitical effects throughout the ancient world.

The Iron Age dates to about 1200 B.C., though it hit different areas at different times. Iron working probably arose first in the Aegean region. The seafaring Phoenicians may have brought these skills to Canaan, where iron rapidly became the monopoly of the Philistines.

Canaan had plenty of iron. In Deuteronomy 8:9 (NIV), Moses referred to the Promised Land as " . . . a land where the rocks are iron and you can dig copper out of the hills."

But only the Philistines knew how to work with iron, and they safely guarded their technology for a couple of centuries. When the Israelites had trouble in their conquest of the land, some complained to Joshua,

" . . . All the Canaanites who live in the plain have iron chariots . . ." (Joshua 17:16 JFB).

First Samuel 13:19-22 (TLB) illustrates the Philistines' continuing dominance in metallurgy in the eleventh century B.C. and the effect on the neighboring Israelites: There were no blacksmiths at all in the land of Israel in those days, for the Philistines would not allow them for fear of their making swords and spears for the Hebrews. So whenever the Israelites needed to sharpen their plowshares, discs, axes, or sickles, they had to take them to a Philistine blacksmith. (The schedule of charges was as follows:

> For sharpening a plow point, 60 c
> For sharpening a disc, 60c
> For sharpening an axe, 30 c
> For sharpening a sickle, 30 c
> For sharpening an ox goad, 30 c

So there was not a single sword or spear in the entire "army" of Israel that day, except for Saul's and Jonathan's.

Fig. 68. Ancient kiln

Fig. 69. A potter's oven at Tell Qasileh

In 3500 B.C., Mesopotamian kilns were constructed with a perforated floor oven, the firebox. In the chamber at right, the potter placed items for baking. This prevented ash and pieces of wood from coming in contact with the surfaces of the vessels, causing defects.

Fig. 70. Section through a copper-casting furnace

A beehive-shaped furnace with a stone stack was placed over a trench to admit combustion air. Clay crucibles containing molten copper stand over a charcoal fire. Air holes in the bottom of the furnace create a draft or provide openings for use of bellows (Cornfeld 1976, 161).

Fig. 71. A beehive-shaped furnace

Fig. 72. An ancient Egyptian furnace

It was only a matter of time before the Israelites learned how to work iron. In David's reign we read of iron axes (2 Samuel 12:31) and of iron nails and fittings stockpiled for the construction of the Temple (1 Chronicles 22:3).

Iron Making

Making iron was relatively simple. Iron ore was crushed and placed in a deep bed of burning charcoal. Carbon from the charcoal would combine with oxygen from the iron ore (iron oxide) and escape as carbon dioxide gas, leaving the iron relatively pure.

Although early metallurgists used hollow tubes to blow on their fires and make them hotter (figure 52), and later ones used bellows, they could not heat the iron to its melting point (about 1,530 degrees centigrade), but they could soften it into a workable, spongy mass called a "bloom." This trapped silica impurities inside, requiring repeated heating and pounding to purify it. Eventually the pure metal would be softer than bronze and could be pounded into a usable shape.

This was "black iron," fairly strong, but still limited in several ways. Forging was a difficult way to purify the metal—and it still retained many impurities. Since it required the hands-on work of pounding and forging, only a small amount of iron could be worked with at a time. The Bible depicts the wearisome work of the blacksmith:

> The blacksmith takes a tool and works with it in the coals; he shapes an idol with hammers, he forges it with the might of his arm. He gets hungry and loses his strength; he drinks no water and grows faint. (Isaiah 44:12 NIV)

> So it is with the smith, sitting by his anvil, intent on his iron-work. The smoke of the fire shrivels his flesh, as he wrestles in the heat of the furnace. The hammer rings again and again in his ears, and his eyes are on the pattern he is copying. He concentrates on completing the task, and stays up late to give it a perfect finish. (Apocrypha; Ecclesiasticus 38:28)

When ironworkers gained the ability to make hotter fires, it greatly improved their product. Black iron was smelted at 800-1,000 degrees centigrade. But at 1,530 degrees centigrade, the iron liquefied. Much freer from impurities, this iron could also be cast in molds. Iron revolutionized warfare, through iron-plated chariots and weapons, and farming with iron spades and plows, but it also made masonry and timber construction more feasible. Iron shafts, nails, dowels, plates, and other fittings created strong connections between other building materials. (See Figures 53-55.)

In addition, one more advance in iron working was made. Heated with charcoal, iron can "carburize," combining with the carbon in the charcoal. If the metal is suddenly dipped in cold water, it becomes steel. Subsequent reheating, or tempering, reduces this metal's brittleness. Some modern scholars theorize that the Spartans owed their success of fifth-century struggles against Persia and Athens to their invention of steel. Their steel weapons would easily outclass the softer wrought iron or bronze weapons of their foes (Muhly 1982, 42-50).

7

Trades, Tools, and Machines

THE QUALITY OF THE ANCIENT INFRASTRUCTURES—THE BUILDINGS, roads, waterworks, and vehicles of society—depended on three factors. First, the builders needed the proper skills. Even though iron was plentiful in Canaan, the Israelites did not know how to forge it into useful implements. They lacked crucial skills.

Second, the workers needed proper tools. Stonemasons required hammers, chisels, plumb lines, and levels. Carpentry developed with the advent of adzes, awls, saws, and metal nails. Metallurgists needed furnaces that could reach high temperatures, often with the aid of bellows, and strong hammers and anvils to forge their products. Tools needed to be strong enough and accurate enough for the tasks at hand.

Finally, the history of civilization shows us the importance of new machinery. Many of the great advances in building and weaponry and transportation came about through the invention of new contraptions that got the job done better. Starting with such simple devices as the block and tackle, derricks, gin poles, levers, and screw jacks, certain innovators got the jump on others through clever use of new machines. The pattern has repeated throughout history.

Quarrying and Stone Masonry

Generally, in biblical times, the craft of masonry—dressing and placing stones—also involved quarrying. In fact, the stones were usually hewn into shape at the quarry.

Stone masonry had its heyday in Israel during the building of Solomon's Temple.

Ancient Tools

Fig. 73. Shaping a flint tool
The use of flint dates back to the Lower Paleolithic period, and this material was probably the first tool crafted by humans. Flakes were chipped off a suitable stone, leaving a rough, dimpled surface that could be used for cutting, chopping, or scraping.

Fig. 74. An early hammer   **Fig. 75. An early adze**

Fig. 76. A plowshare
*Gottlieb Schmacher found this tool
in Megiddo during the excavations in
1903- 1905. The blacksmith's workshop in
which it was found dates from about the tenth
century B.C. (Muhly 1982, 54; Reader's Digest Edit
People 1981.116)*

Fig. 77. A hoe
*This tool was also found at
Megiddo from the same
period.*

Fig. 78. An ox goad
*A third tool was found in the blacksmith's
workshop in Megiddo (Reader's Digest
Editors People 1981, 116).*

Fig. 79. An iron tool
(Muhly 1982, 45)

Fig. 80. An iron pick

This tool was found in Har Adir, in the Upper Galilee, and is from the twelfth or thirteenth century B.C. Laboratory testing of the metal indicated that the tool was made of steel—carburized iron that had been quenched and then tempered.

Fig. 81. A biblical plow

This bronze plowshare and wood tailpiece are similar to those farmers in the Holy Land use today.

Fig. 82. A level

Fig. 83. A carpenter using an ancient saw
*A wood strut separated the saw's two arms, which held a metal blade at one end
and a twisted rope tie at the other. The tie was tightened by twisting the rope with
a tourniquet (Reader's Digest Editorial People 1981, 329).*

Solomon commissioned other building projects besides the Temple.
His own palace took thirteen years to complete and was " . . . made of
blocks of high-grade stone cut to size and trimmed with a saw on their
inner and outer faces" (1 Kings 7:9 NIV).

*Solomon had seventy thousand carriers and eighty thousand stonecutters
in the hills, as well as thirty-three hundred foremen who supervised the
project and directed the workers. At the king's command they removed
from the quarry large blocks of quality stone to provide a foundation of
dressed stone for the temple. (1 Kings 5:15–17 NIV)*

Of course, the Egyptian pyramids, built much earlier, remain the
crowning feat of stone masonry. Those huge stones also tell us more
about the craft. Marks on the stone indicate the use of straight saws, circular saws, and tubular drills with jeweled cutting points. The bronze saw
blades were .003 to .002 of an inch thick.

But stone walls also cross the Judean hills, creating terraces for farming. These walls, which trap the rainfall and retain the soil, represent the work of some of the earliest stonemasons.

Carpentry

The New Testament identifies Jesus as a carpenter (Mark 6:3) and the son of a carpenter (Matthew 13:55). Elsewhere, the Bible frequently mentions carpenters and their tools—dating back to Noah (Genesis 6) and Bezalel, who made the Ark of the Covenant (Exodus 37). Isaiah describes the carpenter's craft: *"The carpenter measures with a line and makes an outline with a marker; he roughs it out with chisels and marks it with compasses . . ."* *(Isaiah 44:13 NIV).*

Later, Jeremiah ironically refers to the hammer and nails a pagan carpenter would use to keep a wooden idol from failing down (Jeremiah 10:4).

Fig. 84. A carving showing Roman tools
This stone carving, found in a tomb of the first century A.D., shows common tools used by the Roman craftsmen, including a ruler, an adjustable triangle, a plumb bob (or plummet) a divider, a compass (or caliper), and a square set.

Machines

Beginning with simple devices—pulleys and levers—builders of the biblical period developed machines that enabled them to expand on their previously available technologies.

WHEELS AND AXLES

The earliest known use of wheel was the potter's wheel, invented in Mesopotamia about 3500 B.C. This flat disc of wood or stone had the center hollowed out on the underside, so it could fit over a stone or hardwood dome set in the ground. The wheel and axle soon followed, revolutionizing transportation. Subsequent developments included the waterwheel and the geared windlass (Landels 1978, 20).

PULLEYS

By using a pulley, an engineer reduces the amount of force required to move a heavy load. A two-block pulley, known as a block and tackle, provides even more advantage. The more pulley wheels applied to a job, the greater the mechanical advantage. A third-century A.D. account describes the pulley's use:

> *If we want to move any weight whatever, we tie a rope to this weight and*
> *. . . pull the rope until we lift it. And for this is needed a power equal to*
> *the weight that we want to lift. But if we untie the rope from the weight,*
> *and tie one of the ends to a solid cross beam and pass its other end*
> *[around] a pulley fastened to the middle of the burden and draw on the*
> *rope, our moving of that weight will be easier (Landels 1978, 4).*

LEVERS

Archimedes extolled the value of simple lever, boldly stating, "Give me a fulcrum on which to rest, and I will move the world." This early Greek engineer explained the mechanical operation of the lever, "Equal weights at unequal distances . . . incline toward the weight which is at the greater distance."

Thus, ancient builders learned they could move large objects easily, with a well-positioned lever (De Camp 1963, 156).

Screws

About 200 B.C., a Greek mathematician, Apollonius of Perga, worked out the geometry of the spiral helix, on which the screw is based. This concept, employed in a screw jack, can be used to lift heavy objects.

Lifting Devices

ROPES

Since ancient times, people have used vegetable material for hauling and lifting loads. First, vines were twisted together to form stronger strands that were still flexible enough for tying knots. Later, other rope materials included the fibrous bark of the palm tree, camel hair, horsehair, leather thongs, jute, sisal, flax, and wild and cultivated hemp.

After cutting individual fibers into roughly seven-foot lengths, rope makers drew them out on frames, which combed out the fibers and made them parallel. Cordage, or special oils, applied in this stage, lubricated and preserved the rope.

The fiber, or slivers, came out in a fluffy stream, and were re-combed six or seven times. During this process, rope makers blended in other fibers of the same grade to ensure a uniform quality. They then spun the fibers into a yarn. This would be twisted, left-handed, into a strand. Three or more strands would then be twisted, right-handed, into the finished rope.

Ancient mariners preferred flaxen rope, as did many builders, hunters, and warriors. Its manufacture involved a team of three in a "rope walk." (See Figure 90.) The rope strands would be stretched tight, with a man at each end and a third in the center. The end of each strand was attached to a tool that was weighted by a stone. At one end a man would begin twirling these stone-laden tools, twisting the strands, while walking toward the center. The man at the other end would back away, twirling in the other direction, while the center man tightened the strands with a spike. Thus the individual fibers twisted in one direction, forming two strands, and these strands were twisted in the opposite direction, forming a single rope (Rossnagel 1964, 14, 15). (See Fig. 90.)

PULLEYS

Fig. 85. A parallel two-sheave block

Fig. 86. A tandem two-sheave block
The side plates on the sheaves are called the cheeks.

Fig. 87. Various block-and-tackle arrangements

The mechanical advantage of each of these pulley arrangements is directly proportional to the number of pulleys involved. Arrows represent the applied pull (Landels 1978, 84).

Fig. 88. Gin pole

This ancient form of rigging employed the pulley concept to haul building stones. Its parts included the mast, which was held in position by guy lines and anchor pegs (or "dead men"), a three-part load line, a two-sheave pulley block, and a single-sheave block (De Camp 1963, 26).

Fig. 89. Forces involved with leverage

A relatively small force at the end of a lever can result in a large force near the pivot point, or fulcrum (Rossnagel 1964, 10).

Fig. 90. Ancient flaxen rope making

The manufacture of flaxen rope required a team of three in a "rope walk." As one man walked forward, twirling weighted strands, another, at the center, controlled the tautness of the rope with spikes; the third man combined the strands by twirling in the opposite direction (Reader's Digest Editors People *1981, 233).*

CRANES AND CAPSTANS

As long as the transportation of building materials relied on simple manpower or animal power, the size of the materials was limited. With the exception of monumental projects like the pyramids, most building stones needed to weigh less than eighty pounds or so. For instance, the columns in early Greek temples (fifth century B.C.) consisted of column drums piled one on top of the other. The weight of monolithic columns would have been prohibitive for transportation using men or animals.

But this changed with the invention of two popular mechanical devices—the capstan (or windlass) and the crane. Ropes and various combinations of pulleys could now multiply the effective force of the workers.

The windlass used the winding of a rope around a rotating drum to exert force for lifting. At first, handspikes inserted into the drum did the winding. Later, workers used cranks, which generally had less power but greater speed. Sometimes the handspikes were long enough that several men could turn simultaneously, developing great power. To prevent a backlash, the windlass sometimes had a ratchet-type device that kept the cylinder from rotating backwards.

Vitruvius described the set-up and workings of a basic A-frame and windlass-pulley system:

> Two timbers must be provided, strong enough to withstand the weight of the load, and they must be fastened together at the upper end by a bolt; then they are spread apart at the bottom, thus set up and kept upright by ropes attached to the upper ends and fixed at suitable intervals all around.

A block is fastened at the top [called a "rechamus"]. Two sheaves [pulleys] are enclosed in the block, turning on axles. The traction rope is carried over the top sheave, then let fall and passed around the sheave in the block below. It is then brought back to the sheave at the bottom of the upper block and thus goes down to the lower block; it is fastened there through a hole in the block.

> The other end of the block is pulled back and down through the legs of the hoisting machine.

> Socket pieces are nailed to the hinder faces of the squared timbers at point where they are placed apart; the ends of the windlass are also inserted into them. Two holes are made close to the windlass so that the axles may turn freely and so adjusted that the handspikes can be fitted into them.

> Shears made of iron are fastened to the bottom of the lower block, and their prongs are brought to bear upon the stones. The latter must have suitable holes bored into them. As one end of the rope fastens to the windlass—and the latter is turned around by working the hand spikes—the rope winds around the windlass, becomes tightly drawn, and thus raises the heavy loads to the heights desired in the work.

. . . When we must provide machines for heavier loads, we should use timbers of greater length and thickness, and be sure to provide them with corresponding large bolts at the top, as well as windlasses for turning at the bottom. When these are provided, let forestays be attached, then let left lying slack in front; carry the backstays over the shoulders of the machine to some distance; if there is nothing to which they may be fastened, sloping piles may be driven, the ground rammed down hard all around to fix them firmly, and the ropes made fast to them.

A block should then be attached by very stout cord to the top of the machine and from that point a rope (is) carried to the pile. The rope should be put around the sheave of this block, then brought to the block that is fastened to the top (of the machine). The rope should be passed around its sheave and then go down from the top and back to the windlass, which is at the bottom of the machine; it should then be fastened.

The windlass must now be turned by means of handspikes, and it will raise the machine without any danger. A machine of the larger type will now be set in position, with its ropes in their place about it, and its stays attached to the piles (Morgan 1960, 295).

Fig. 91. A simple A-frame

Fig. 92. An A-frame and windlass

This simple hoisting rig included a timber A-frame, fastened by an iron bolt at the apex and held upright by ropes. From this was suspended a double-pulley block and a lower single-pulley block. The hoisting rope was wound by a windlass (De Camp 1963, 26).

Fig. 93. Stick capstan

Capstan

Drum

Strongback

Pile anchor

Fig. 94. Anchor and capstan

Fig. 95. A derrick

Fig. 96. & 97. Ancient treadwheels

To provide power for screw pumps, ancient man used treadwheels. Above you see the treadwheel alone. The complete device included a platform, or base, an inclined jib with a bracket that held the rotating shaft, a drum, and the tread-wheel (De Camp 1963, 193).

Fig. 98. A millstone for crushing olives

With this device, a man or animal could crush or grind olives or other materials to extract oil. As it rolls around the basin, the stone crushes and squeezes the fruit.

TREADMILLS

The treadmill, or tread wheel, further harnessed human and animal power for lifting, turning, and pulling. By climbing the "rungs" of a vertically placed wheel, a man could use his own weight to turn the wheel and pull or hoist whatever it was attached to. The treadmill also offered greater mobility. A combination treadmill and crane could be dismantled—the jib could be laid horizontally on one or more carts, and the wheel could be rolled along the roadway.

With such machines, ancient builders hoisted huge blocks—ashlars weighing tens of tons—and precisely placed them in position. While some earlier wonders of construction, such as the pyramids and Solomon's Temple, used thousands of forced laborers, even these builders used primitive machines and methods to multiply the effective force of their manpower. As time went on, machines enabled fewer workers to do more work.

As early as the first century A.D., the Roman Emperor Vespasian feared that mechanization might cause unemployment. An engineer offered to haul some huge columns up to the Capitol at a moderate expense by a simple mechanical device, but Vespasian declined his services, saying, "I must always ensure that the working class earn enough money to buy themselves food." Nevertheless he paid the engineer a very handsome fee (De Camp 1963, 170).

Fig. 99. A donkey mill
Usually a donkey would power this mill, thus the name it bears. Raw materials were loaded into the upper cone. As the donkey turned the mill, the material would fall between the faces on the lower parts of the cone. The modern-day gyratory crusher, used in mills to reduce the size of ore, is a more sophisticated version of this mill (De Camp 1963, 244).

Fig. 100. Transporting a log by donkey

Fig. 101.

The end of a boom

The full assembly included the rope, pulley, or sheave, upper block with a single sheave, lower block with two sheaves, and the load hook. The mechanical advantage of the depicted arrangement is 4:1—therefore, a 100-pound pull on the rope could lift 400 pounds.

Fig. 102. A guyed double-mast derrick

Fig. 103. A guyed single-mast derrick powered with a treadwheel

Fig. 104. Forces involved in transporting heavy stone blocks

The force required moving the load up a slight incline is only a small fraction of the weight of the stone.

Fig. 105. One method of moving large stone blocks

With moveable wooden rails and rollers, set progressively under a stone block, workmen may have moved each block of limestone that made up Cheops's pyramid; blocks weighed up to 2.5 tons. As the men pulled the ropes, they applied leverage to one end of the stone (Reader's Digest Editors People *1981, 359).*

Fig. 106. Rolling a stone block

Fig. 107. Transporting large stone blocks on rollers

Fig. 108. Moving stone blocks with pulleys

Fig. 109. Chord method for moving stone

Fig. 110. Moving a stone block

Fig. 111. Rolling a stone cylinder

Fig. 112. Moving a stone drum

Fig. 113. Rolling a column

Fig. 114. One theory about erecting an obelisk

Fig. 115. How obelisks may have been transported

The workers pull on ropes attached to the stone shaft. Below the stone lie wooden rails and rollers, dampened with water to reduce friction. As foremen clap their hands or beat on drums, the workers rhythmically pull their lines.

Fig. 116. Lifting a stone block with a hook

Fig. 117. Ancient hook devices

In about 800 B.C., the Greeks used these hooks for lifting heavy stone blocks.
Mortises, or bored holes, cut into the stone face allowed the use of various types
of anchors. The complete assembly included the lower load block, iron shears or
forceps, and prongs (Landels 1981, 84).

Fig. 118. Erecting an obelisk on a foundation

Although no one knows how Hatshepsut's Obelisk was raised, many have speculated how this feat of engineering might have been accomplished. Henri Cherier hypothesized that first a stone foundation and pedestal were built, and then an earthen ramp was formed atop the pedestal. To place the obelisk, workers might have pulled the stone shaft to the top, using rollers and rails. When they had placed the butt end almost over the pedestal, they could begin excavating a pit. Slowly this would have rotated the obelisk to its vertical placement, and it would finally have rested on the pedestal.

Alternatively, a tunnel might have been excavated to the pedestal and the sand might have been removed, causing a pit down which workmen might have rotated the obelisk.

Whichever method the Egyptian workmen used, they had to use precise techniques to control such a huge object.

**Fig. 119.
Driving a pile
with a mandrel**

Narrow part of pile

Mandrel

Work platform

Pile

Guy line

Deadman

Maul

Pile

Driven Piles

Platform

**Fig. 120. Driving a pile
with a maul**

Fig. 121. Driving a pile with a mandrel and A-frame

Fig. 122. Excavating the Temple Mount

Fig. 123. Setting a stone lintel

Fig. 124. Using an A-frame for raising a stone block

8

Prominent Engineers of History

Archimedes

THE GREEK ENGINEER AND MATHEMATICIAN, *ARCHIMEDES*, IS best known for his discovery of the principle of flotation. A body in water, he said, has three natural states: Its density is equal to, less than, or greater than the surrounding liquid.

Herod's engineers were doubtlessly familiar with Archimedes's scholarly writings. Archimedes of Syracuse combined mathematics, mechanics, and hydrostatics. In his *Principle of Archimedes*, he wrote the basic laws of ship design:

"The upward thrust on a body immersed in a fluid equals the weight of the fluid displaced by the body."

"The three natural states of a body in water are: a body whose density is equal to, less than and greater than, that of a liquid in which it was immersed."

"A body less dense than the liquid would float, and the portion of it which is submerged has the same ratio to the whole volume of the body as its whole weight had to that of an equal volume of water."

"If the body is forcibly held below the surface, it will exert an upward force equal to the difference between its own weight and the liquid it displaced."

Archimedes' principles remain the basis of ship design to the present day.

Vitruvius

You might call Vitruvius the founding father of architecture. His ten-book series, *De Architectura* (On Architecture), written for Roman Emperor Augustus, dealt with the rebuilding of Rome after its ruinous civil war of the first century B.C. In these books, Vitruvius laid the ground rules for the architect's work (Landels 1978, 36, 208).

The word architect comes from Greek words for the "supervisor" or "coordinator of various craftsmen." In Book 1, Vitruvius explains the basic knowledge necessary for such a coordinator.

He dedicated his books to the rebuilding of Rome after the Civil War, which was concurrent with the beginning of the Herodian Period. Each of his *Ten Books* contained the following:

Book I was an encyclopedia of knowledge required for the architect.

Book II was the history of building developments, starting with the primitive mud huts to contemporary building materials. It included sun-dried and kiln-dried brick, *pozzolana*, marble, *tufa* (a soft volcanic rock), and sandstone building blocks.

Books III and IV covered site development, design and decoration of temples, including the Doric, Ionic, and Corinthian Orders.

Book V described public buildings and facilities, such as forums, basilica, and baths.

Book VI reported on the relationship between climate and building design.

Book VII was about internal and external decoration, stucco, and coloring materials.

Books VIII, IX, and X were mainly on water supply, astronomy, optics, and mechanical devices. These devices included cranes, water pumps, water wheels, catapults, and other siege engines. Here, Vitruvius described how to arm *ballistas, catapults,* and *scorpions* by tuning them to a proper musical key. (De Camp 1963, 27) He also told how to design the frames, twisted sinew, and windlasses of battle engines.

Frontinus

Sextus Julius Frontinus specialized in water supply and engineering. Born in A.D. 35, he held his first political office in A.D. 70. In A.D. 97 he was responsible for the water-supply system for all of Rome, under Emperor Nerva. Frontinus was in charge of a total labor force of 700, including overseers, reservoir keepers, stonemasons, plasterers, and others. He personally inspected all water-supply projects throughout the Roman Empire (Landels 1978, 21).

Thales

Herod's engineers were also acquainted with the works of Thales of Miletus. Thales was an Ionic philosopher of the sixth century B.C. He was a military advisor and wrote about the natural science of the universe and practical techniques for measuring angles.

Hero of Alexandria

For machine design, Herod's engineers looked to *Hero,* who lived in the first century and studied the theories of Archimedes. *Hero's Mechanics* was a complete treatise on the theory and application of practical mechanics. This manuscript served as an engineering manual and described the five elementary machines: windlass, lever, pulley, wedge, and the worm gear. He also explained the *gear ratio* and its implications, the *parallelogram of forces*, and the block and tackle arrangements.

Another of Hero's works was *Pneumatica,* which discussed the properties of air, behavior of liquids and the impossibility of a continuous vacuum. Hero's *Pneumatica* explained why a liquid flows through a siphon. He was a student of earlier technical writers, Strato of Lampsacus and Ctesibius.

Hero's books on *Metrica* dealt with pure geometry, plane figures, triangles, and segments of circles. He explained surveying and the use of instruments, sightings, and water levels for alignment. Based on Hero's books, surveyors used vertical poles with movable marker discs to find relative heights at various points of the ground.

Hero's writings involved both mechanics and warfare. These became the bases of investigation in the *School of Alexandria.* Topics included *geodesy,* the science of measurement of the earth's surface, *automata,* the science of moving machines, and *baraclcus,* the science of traction of heavy weights. Also included were the sciences of weights and measures, metrology, measuring instruments, lenses, mirrors, pneumatics, and waterpower.

The titles of Hero's books were:

- *Pneumatica* on air and liquids

- *Automatopoietike* on automatic devices

- *Mechanica* on machinery

- *Catoptrica* on mirrors

- *Metrica* on pure geometry

- *Dioptra* on surveying

- *Geometrica, Sereometrica* on solid geometry

- *Belopoeca* on catapult construction

- *Cheiroballistra* on hand-catapults

Pliny

Gaius Plinius Secundus is known to history as Pliny the Elder, distinguishing him from his nephew, who became a Roman governor. Born in A.D. 23, he became chief of fleet under Emperor Vespasian in A.D. 69.

But Pliny was primarily a scholar. In thirty-seven rolls, or books, of papyrus, Pliny set forth his *Historia Naturalis* (Natural History), in which he claimed there were more than 20,000 important facts.

Although Pliny wrote his treatises soon after the end of the Herodian Period, his works showed the state of mathematics and science of the time. His writings contained the following subjects:

- Book 1 indexed topics and sources.

- Book 2 covered the universe, stars, planets, and astronomy.

- Books 3 to 6 described the world geography.

- Books 7 to 11 covered human and animal anatomy.

- Books 12 to 32 included botany and medical substances.

- Books 33 to 37 described mineral substances, including metals, stones, mining, metallurgy, and the use of these materials in medicine, painting and architecture. (Casson, The Ancient Mariners, 1959)

9

Measurements, Mathematics, and Geometry

First Development of Writing

T HE INVENTION OF CUNEIFORM WRITING IN BABYLONIA WAS A first in the ancient world and lasted 3000 years. It was adapted for many different languages throughout Western Asia. Although developed by early Sumerians for administrative purposes, it was adapted by their successors for religious writing, literary works, mathematics, and science. The Sumerian and Babylonian achievements were later built upon by subsequent civilizations in Western Asia and Europe.

Numerals

Babylonians used the cuneiform for figures, characters, and groups of figures to express a number. Figure 125 shows some of these ancient

characters and numerals. These symbols are wedge-shaped like **V** or **<**
as shown below:

$$\textbf{V} \quad = \quad \textbf{1}$$

$$\textbf{VV} \quad = \quad \textbf{2}$$

$$\textbf{VVV} \quad = \quad \textbf{3}$$

$$\begin{matrix} \textbf{VVV} \\ \textbf{V} \end{matrix} \quad = \quad \textbf{4}$$

$$\begin{matrix} \textbf{VVV} \\ \textbf{VV} \end{matrix} \quad = \quad \textbf{5}$$

$$\begin{matrix} \textbf{VVV} \\ \textbf{VVV} \end{matrix} \quad = \quad \textbf{6}$$

$$\begin{matrix} \textbf{VVV} \\ \textbf{VVV} \\ \textbf{V} \end{matrix} \quad = \quad \textbf{7}$$

$$\begin{matrix} \textbf{VVV} \\ \textbf{VVV} \\ \textbf{VV} \end{matrix} \quad = \quad \textbf{8}$$

$$\begin{matrix} \textbf{VVV} \\ \textbf{VVV} \\ \textbf{VVV} \end{matrix} \quad = \quad \textbf{9}$$

$$\textbf{<} \quad = \quad \textbf{10}$$

Fig. 125. Mathematics and numerals

This figure shows the evolution of writing from the Early Assyrians, through Babylonian, to Greek. This started with marking in wet clay to carving in stone, and finally led to writing with ink on papyrus.

The Romans used letters to represent numerals to define certain quantities. For example:

$$
\begin{array}{ccc}
\text{I} & = & 1 \\
\text{V} & = & 5 \\
\text{X} & = & 10 \\
\text{L} & = & 50 \\
\text{C} & = & 100 \\
\text{D} & = & 500 \\
\text{M} & = & 1000 \\
\end{array}
$$

Double letters represented set values, such as:

$$IV = 4$$
$$IX = 9$$

A bar drawn over the letters meant that the quantity was to be multiplied by 1000, such as

$$\overline{XIII} = 13,000$$

There was no letter for zero.

Alternatively, full combinations of letters represented the following:

$$MMDCCLXIII = 2763$$

Where:

$$MM = 1000 + 1000$$
$$DCC = 500 + 100 + 100$$
$$LX = 60$$
$$III = 3$$

Mathematics

The early Sumerians used clay tablets for record keeping. They pressed a rounded or pointed stick on the surface of wet clay blocks, which formed circular, semicircular, or wedge-shaped characters. The blocks were then baked by fire or in the sun.

The Babylonian and Greek mathematics were used to measure land and quantities of materials. They inscribed symbols and numerals on cuneiform tablets for multiplication tables, reciprocals, and square roots.

The Babylonians used a *sexagesimal* system with a base 60 to measure time and degrees of a circle. For example, one hour was divided into 60 minutes and one minute into 60 seconds.

From the fifth century B.C. to the fifth century A.D., Greek mathematicians had a tradition of exact sciences. This included mathematics, astronomy, and related fields. Euclid's *Elements*, written in 300 B.C., was a treatise on geometry, proportions, and the theory of numbers. As an example, the *Pythagorean Theorem*:

> *"The square of the hypotenuse of a right triangle is equal to the sum of the squares of the sides."*

Based on this theorem, the Biblical engineers knew that a triangle with sides of three, four, and five cubits would form a right triangle. They used this rule to layout a square or a rectangular building as shown in Figure 126.

Fig. 126. **Squaring building lines**
This simple way of making square corners of a building was by using the 3-4-5 right triangle. In this case, the sides of the triangle were 30 and 40 cubits giving a hypotenuse equal to 50 cubits.

As early as 1800 B.C., Babylonians inscribed banking calculations in cuneiform script on clay tablets. The *Hammurobic Code of Laws* was also written in cuneiform about 2100 B.C.

Merchants used wax tablets and abacuses to add, subtract, and multiply.

The Quadratum Geometricum   3-4-5 Right Triangle

Roman Abacus

Fig. 127. Calculating devices
Ancient people used the abacus for adding, multiplying, and dividing numbers

They also employed inscribed tablets, which contained squares of numbers from one to 60 and cubes of numbers from one to 32. A square of a number is the product of that number times itself. As an example, the *square* of 5 is 25, or 5 times 5. Similarly, a *cube* of a number is the product of that number times itself twice. An example is the cube of 4 is 64, or 4 times 4 times 4. The Greeks, Romans, and Judeans commonly used the abacus for multiplication.

Mathematicians could prove formulas by lines and rectangles without using algebraic shorthand. As example, they could prove the *Quadratic Equation* $(a + b)^2 = a^2 + 2ab + b^2$ by drawing a set of rectangles.

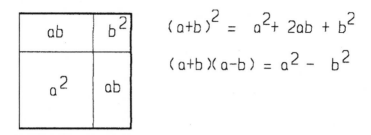

$$(a+b)^2 = a^2 + 2ab + b^2$$

$$(a+b)(a-b) = a^2 - b^2$$

Fig. 128. Quadratic equation

The proof of the quadratic equation was given by the total area $(a+b)^2$ was equal to the areas of four squares, each equaled the values of ab, b^2, and a^2 .

An important branch of mathematics required by early surveyors and builders was *geometry*. This term was from the Greek words "earth" and "to measure."

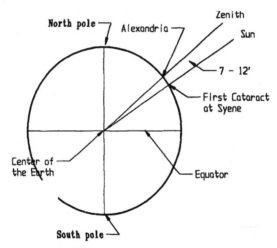

Fig. 129. Eratosthenes's diagram

This diagram shows how Eratosthenes *estimated the earth diameter by employing mathematical theories, geometrical methods, and the course of the sun. He found that the sun at noon was exactly in the zenith at Syene (First Cataract of the Nile) when it was 7 degrees 12 minutes south of the zenith at Alexandria. Since the distance between the two points was 5000 stadia, he calculated that the earth's diameter was 7850 miles. This was only 50 miles less than the polar diameter, as we know it. (Smith, History of Mathematics)*

Although some early Hebrew inscriptions contain symbols that may be numerals, the Hebrew language has always counted on the letters of its alphabet to serve double duty as numbers. The first nine letters, *aleph* through *tet*, stand for the numbers one to nine. The tenth letter, *yod*, is ten, and the following letters are twenty, thirty, forty, and so on. The last four letters, *kof* to *tav,* are hundreds, 100 to 400. Of course, combinations of these letters form other numbers. Eleven would be *yod aleph*, ten plus one. Two interesting exceptions are fifteen and sixteen, which were not written *yod he* and *yod vav*, as you would expect. Those were shortened forms of God's name. Instead, these were written as nine plus six (*tet vav*) and nine plus seven (*tet zayin*).

Ancient man could also do more complicated calculations. In 1800 B.C., a Babylonian inscribed a clay tablet with a banking calculation, in cuneiform script. This writing was an algorithm, or step-by-step procedure for solving a specific problem, similar to modern computer programming. The scribe explained the procedure by presenting an example. Others could substitute the appropriate numbers for their own calculations. This procedure determined how many years and months it would take to double a certain quantity of grain (grain served as currency) at an annual interest rate of 20 percent.

Measurements

Ancient Egyptians measured distances in units equal to parts of the human body, as did many early societies. The finger was generally the smallest unit. Four fingers equaled one hand. Three hands made a span (the distance from the tip of the little finger to the tip of the thumb, when the hand is stretched out). Two spans made a cubit (the length of the forearm)

The Babylonians based their six-decimal system on a linear unit from astronomical calculations. This system was broadly accepted throughout the Middle East.

In Palestine, both the Egyptian and the Babylonian systems were used. The Hebrews, who had used the Babylonian system, introduced changes as a result of Egyptian influence. The Phoenicians and Persians added later changes. Thus the measurements mentioned in Scripture reflect varying standards.

The Persians had a distance measurement similar to the mile. It was 1,000 fathoms (2,000 yards) long. The word mile actually derives from the Latin *mille passuum,* "a thousand paces." The ancient Roman pace consisted of two steps, or about five feet. So 1,000 paces would equal about 5,000 feet, close to our statute mile of 5280 feet. The Romans divided their mile into eight *stadia* of about 208 yards each (Brown 1962, 67-69).

Length Measurements

As noted above, most ancient societies used parts of the body as units of measurement. Accurate lengths became important when people began to divide land. As long as rough measurements were adequate, the dimensions of a man's body, the breadth of the palm, lengths of the forearm, distance of the stride, and height, were satisfactory. But these units of measurement had to be standardized for accuracy. Consequently, royal cubits were made into standard units by Egyptian, Sumerian, Assyrian, Greek, Persian, and Roman rulers.

Some of the units used for measurements of length and weight differed in the Old and New Testament. Their values also differed in other societies. For example, a *cubit* was the distance from the tip of the middle finger to the elbow (Deuteronomy 3:11). Equivalent to two *spans*, a cubit was equal to:

> 17.49 inches in the Old Testament
> 18 inches in the New Testament
> 20.6 inches in Egypt 3000 BC
> 19.5 inches in Sumeria
> 18.2 inches in Greece
> 525 mm to 530 mm
> 4 palms or 24 digits

A span was the distance from the tip of the middle finger to the tip of the thumb with the fingers spread. This was equivalent to three *handbreadths*, and equal to 8.745 inches. Additional units of measurement included:

- A *handbreadth* was equivalent to 4 fingers and was equal to 2.915 inches.
- *Fingerbreadth* was equal to 1 finger or .728 inches.
- *Two fingers* was equal to 2 finger-widths or 2 *digits*
- *One finger* was equal to a finger-width or 1 *digiti*
- One *hand* or *palm,* or 4 digits
- A *fathom* was equivalent to a man's height, also equal to 72 inches, 4 cubits, or the distance between fingertips with arms outstretched.
- A *range* was the distance that a bow could shot an arrow *(Gen 21:6).*
- A *short distance* was a 2-hour *journey (Gen 35:16, 48:17, 2 Kings 5:19).*
- A *long distance* was a day's journey *(Gen 30:36, 31:23).*
- A *mile,* as used by the Persians, was 1000 fathoms long. (The word *mile* came from the Latin words *mille passuum,* which meant *a thousand paces.)*
- The Roman *pace* consisted of 2 steps (about 5 feet).
- One *land mile* was equal to 1000 paces, 5280 feet, 8 *stadias* or 1665 yards
- One *mile* was equal to 1000 units or 1000 double steps, or 8 *stadia*
- One *foot* was equal to 295.7 mm or 13½ digits

Josephus also described Jewish measures as follows:

- Standard cubit: 1 cubit   21 inches
- Zereth, or large span: 1⁄2 cubit   10.5 inches
- Small span: 1/3 cubit   7 inches
- Palm, or hand breath: 1/6 cubit   3.5 inches
- Inch, or thumb breadth: 1/18 cubit   1.16 inches
- Digit, or finger width: 1/24 cubit   .875 inch
- Fathom: 4 cubits   84 inches
- Schoenus, or line: 80 cubits   140 feet
- Jewish mile: 4000 cubits   7000 feet
- Stadium, or furlong: 1/10 400 cubits   700 feet

Josephus described measurements of dry volumes as follows:

- Bushel: about 1 peck
- Cab, or kab: about 2 quarts
- Ephah: 3 seah, and in liquid, to a bath, containing about 1 1/2 bushel
- Half-homer: about 5 1/2 bushels
- Homer: about 11 bushels, a cor or 10 ephah
- Omer: about 1 bushel
- Seah: about 1 1/2 peck
- Tenth deal: about 1 gallon, 1/10 of an ephah

Measurements of liquid volumes were given as follows:

- Bath: about 8 1/2 gallons
- Firkin: nearly 9 gallons
- Hin: about 1 1/2 gallon
- Log: about 1 pint, 1/12 of a hin

Some Old Testament weights were given as follows:

- Talent (60 Minas): 75.558 grams
- Mina (50 shekels): 20.148 oz.
- Shekel (2 bekas): 176.29 grains
- Beka (10 gerahs): 88.14 grains
- Gerah: 8.81 grains

Vitruvius recognized the importance of devices used for standardizing and measuring weights in the following:

> *"The discovery of the method of testing weights by steel yards and balances saves us from fraud, by introducing honest practices into life."*

As was noted before, most measurements given in the Bible are approximate. The size of Solomon's Temple in the *Book of Ezekiel* is an example. The smallest measurement is one cubit and the largest is 500 cubits. The dimensions of the Temple were given in a dream to Ezekiel, as measured by a "biblical surveyor" (man or angel) "whose appearance was like bronze, with a line of flax and measuring reed in his hand." Errors in long measurements could be plus or minus 100 cubits (155 feet) and in small measurements, errors could be plus or minus one cubit.

Geometry and Surveying

Geometry was originally developed by the Egyptians to determine the size of their fields and reset the boundaries of their farms each year after the Nile flooded. Thus, thousands of years ago, they already practiced an early form of surveying (Brown 1962, 68).

Throughout the ancient world, as nomadic tribes settled down and plotted out their ground, they needed accurate ways of measuring it. Even before the Israelites settled in Canaan, the Law spelled out the sacredness of boundary markers:

> Cursed is the man who removes his neighbor's boundary stone. (Deuteronomy 27:17 NIV)

> Thou shalt not remove thy neighbour's landmark, which they of old time have set in thine inheritance, which thou shalt inherit in the land that the Lord thy God giveth thee to possess it. (Deuteronomy 19:14 KJV)

> Some remove the landmarks; they violently take away flocks, and feed thereof. (Job 24:2 KJV)

Ancient Egyptians also used geometry to resurvey the boundaries of their farms after the annual Nile flooding.

Herodotus, a Greek writer of the fifth century BC, wrote that King Sesostris used geometry in the following quotation:

> "The king divided the land among all Egyptians so that to each he gave a quadrangle of equal size."

The art of surveying was well advanced before the building of the Temple Mount in Jerusalem. Engineers knew how to find the properties and dimensions of circles, cubes, cylinders, ellipses, hexagons, and spheres. Military engineers used this technology in the design and operation of catapults.

Many of the Sumerian and Mesopotamian written records concerned commerce and property surveys. Their numbering system, called *sexagesimal*, combined 10 with 6 to obtain the base figure 60. Using this system, the Sumerians were able to divide into fractions, multiply into millions, calculate roots, and raise numbers to several powers. The 360-degree circle, the foot of 12 inches, and the *dozen* are examples of the *Sumerian Mathematics*.

Methods of Measurement

Excavation of ancient cities indicates that those civilizations already knew a great deal about city planning and laying out the land. The Babylonians divided the circle into 360 degrees, a degree into sixty minutes, and a minute into sixty seconds.

But it took Greek mathematicians to begin developing the reasoning and logic needed to prove the truth of mathematical statements. Thales of Miletus (640-546 B.C.) began the study of lines and triangles. Pythagoras (580-500 B.C.) developed the theorem that bears his name, a way to determine the relative lengths of the sides of right triangles. Plato (427-347 B.C.) developed a logical method of forming a proof, and Aristotle (384-322 B.C.) noted the difference between axioms and postulates. Archimedes (287-212 B.C.) determined volumes and areas by methods now used in calculus.

Herodotus credited a king named Sesostris with the invention of geometry. But the Greek mathematician Euclid is generally considered the father of geometry, because he organized this form of mathematics into a single logical system. His book *The Elements* remains the foundational text in this field.

Geometric calculations gained importance as the complexity of life increased. Not only were more complex buildings being built, but increasingly warfare became waged with machines. A society's survival might depend not only on the strength of its warriors, but also on the accuracy of its mathematicians.

Fig. 130.
Roman steelyard
Ancient Romans used another form of the balance, including a hook, a beam marked with graduations, a fixed weight, and a suspended pan for the unknown weight.

Fig. 131. Determining the weight of floating objects
Archimedes discovered that a floating body displaced its own weight in water.

Surveying and Mapmaking

Herod's surveyors measured distances with a high degree of accuracy. They made both topographic and construction surveys which were necessary for the design and building of the Temple Mount. These surveyors employed geometry and trigonometry, and they recorded the data on papyrus sheets. They set survey stakes in the field at the corners of the proposed structures.

Horizontal planes and right angles were made with an instrument known as the *libra, libella* or *chorobate*. Other measuring devices mentioned in the Bible were the thread *(Jer 52:21)*, rope *(Amos 7:17)*, measuring or flax line *(Zech 2:5, Jer 31:38)*, and the measuring reed *(Ezek 40:3)*.

The art of surveying was important even at the time of Abraham. The Bible describes how the Lord spoke to Abraham giving the land to him and his heirs.

> *And Abraham harkened onto Ephron; and Abraham weighed to Ephron the silver, which he had named in the audience of the sons of Heth, four hundred shekels of silver current money with the merchant. On the field of Ephron which was in Machpelah, which was before Mamre, the field, and the cave which were therein, and all the trees, that were in the field, that were in all the borders round about, were made sure unto Abraham for a possession in the presence of the children of Heth, before all that went in the gate of his city (Genesis 23:16-18 KJV).*

In 2000 B.C., in ancient Mesopotamia, clay tables were used to record surveys in which areas were divided into rectangles and triangles. These tablets contained measurements and statistics for specific property.

A survey team included a note keeper, rodman, and two chainmen, who set points and marked distance with a measuring line (Brown 1962, 68, 69).

Fig. 132. Ancient land surveyors at work

Fig. 133. Using a biblical plane table

Fig. 134. Ancient Egyptian rodman

Fig. 135. A Hebrew scribe

A scribe was usually a person that composed and recorded private, public, and religious documents and was also a professional student of Mosaic Law.

Fig. 136. Measuring a cubit length

As the basic cubit was the distance from the fingertip to the elbow, a rope wound around the forearm measured roughly measured this length.

Fig. 137. Using a measuring rope

Markers indicating cubits were attached to a rope give the surveyor a method of measuring distances.

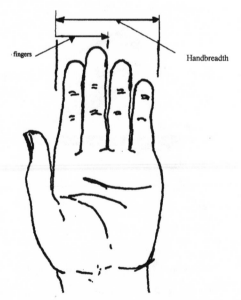

fingers

Handbreadth

Fig. 138. Handbreadth

Small distances were measured by the parts of the hand. For example: handbreadth, two fingers, and the inch, or measure of the thumb from the joint to the tip.

Fig. 139. How the value of pi was determined

A point marked on the rim of the wheel that rotated once was found to travel a distance on the ground that measured 3.14, or pi, times the wheel's diameter.

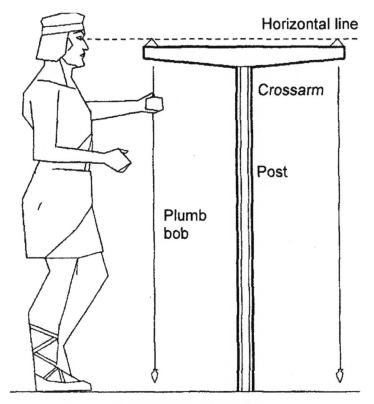

Fig. 140. A biblical transit

Fig. 141. A compass

Writing Materials

Clay Tablets

In addition to papyrus, parchment, and potsherds, scribes wrote on clay tablets. They used wet, clean-washed clay that they rolled smooth and flat, and while still wet, inscribed in wedge-shaped letters with a stylus. The tablet was then dried in the sun or in a kiln. They used this method for books and records that were stored in libraries. One of the most famous is the *Code of Hammurabi* and other law books.

Tablets were made in various shapes—cone-shaped, drum-shaped, and flat. They are practically imperishable; fire only hardens them more. They were the common media for personal and business letters, legal document books, and communications between rulers.

Letters were written on a small slab of wet clay, folded to enclose the message, and the addressee's name written on the outside. The letter was then dried in the same way as a tablet. The recipient of the letter merely had to crack open the letter to read the message.

The Egyptians, Greeks, and Romans used papyrus as their most common writing material. With it, they prepared manuscripts and commercial documents from the fourth century B.C. to the fourth century A.D.

They made papyrus sheets from the pith of plants they had sliced into longitudinal strips. After laying these strips side by side into rectangular units, they superimposed another mat with the strips running at right angles to the former. They added water and glue, and then applied pressure, converting the layers into a homogeneous mass, which they dried, polished, and made ready for use.

Ink, in Biblical times, was a solution of charcoal, or soot, and diluted gum. Jeremiah 36:18 referred to ink, as follows:

> *"So Baruch explained that Jeremiah had dictated them to him word by word, and he had written them down in ink upon the scroll."*

Scribes used an inkhorn with a small hollow receptacle for ink. They carried this in an oblong case with the reed pens. The case was usually worn like a dagger, thrust behind the scribe's girdle.

It was customary to write treatises on long strips of parchment or papyrus. Separate parts of a manuscript were rolled up and called *volumes*, from the Latin root "to roll." When the rolls became too large, they were cut into smaller rolls, or *biblia*, meaning "books" in Greek. As examples, *Books of the Bible* and *Books of Homer.*

Summary

In summary, recorded Biblical history was concurrent with the work of early mathematicians and scientists, as shown in the following chart:

B.C.

2100	Hammurabi invokes building laws
1650	Ahmes, an Egyptian scribe, writes a book on mathematics
1250	Ugarit uses the alphabet
600	Thales demonstrates geometry
540	Pythagorus describes geometry and the theory of numbers
460	Hippocrates of Chios writes on geometry
450	Herodotus, historian
404	Plato establishes foundation of mathematics

340	Aristotle, application of mathematics, logic
336	Alexander the Great establishes the Macedonian Empire
335	Eudemus
334	Alexander in Asia
320	Decarchies
300	Euclid, geometry
287	Gauls invade Macedonia and Greece
270	Strato of Lampsacus
225	Archimedes, geometry, mechanics
220	Rome increasing its strength
146	Greece and Macedonia becomes part of the Roman province
140	Hipparchus writes on astronomy and trigonometry
	Hero and Ptolemy write on astronomy, geography and optics
75	Cicero
48	Julius Caesar defeats Pompey
42	Antonia and Octavian defeat Caesar who is murdered by Brutus
31	Augustus ruler of Rome

A.D.

30	Aitruvius Frontinus
10	Strabo, history of mathematics
50	Hero of Alexandria, geodesy, mathematics
	Pliny
	Plutarch
	Aristaeus

10

Weapons, Fortresses, and Siege Engines

IN THE ANCIENT WORLD, AS TODAY, PEOPLE CONTINUALLY DEVELOPED new kinds of weapons, and each new measure in warfare was counteracted by something more powerful. As measure was followed by countermeasure and counter-countermeasure, both defensive and offensive weapons became increasingly sophisticated. War has always bred better machines.

The Assyrian Army

The Assyrian army ruled Assyria hundreds of years before the Roman legions conquered the ancient world. Assyrian forces triumphed over enemies through a combination of highly skilled troops, superior weapons, and strict discipline. Their soldiers were tough peasant farmers recruited from the rugged highlands of northern Babylonia, who served as conscripts to conquer their enemies for over 300 years. But as the empire grew and its enemies became stronger, a permanent army was needed. King Tiglathpileser III (745-727 B.C.) enlisted fighters from the outlying provinces of the empire, horsemen from Iran, camel drivers from Arabia, and infantrymen from Anatolia and Syria, to form a fulltime standing army. Citizens of Assyria were still liable to be conscripted, but they could send slaves to fight in their place. Later, the army relied on mercenaries from hostile tribes who were attracted by the promise of rich booty. These elements weakened the army and contributed to its eventual defeat.

The number of soldiers engaged in battle was immense. At one battle, King Ashurnasirpal mentioned 50,000 men, and Shalmaneser claimed to have 120,000 men in the field in the Battle of Qarqar in 853 B.C. The carved reliefs in the royal palaces depict the importance of the engineer corps, invaluable for besieging hostile, fortified towns. These men filled in moats, constructed earthworks, dug tunnels, and used enormous battering rams to breach gates or walls.

The infantry consisted of archers and slingers, who had no defensive weapons, and lancers who were protected by coats of mail and tall shields. Cavalrymen, armed with a small bow or a long spear, initially rode bareback, but later their horses were protected by armor. Fast, light, two-wheeled chariots were used, enabling the Assyrians to outmaneuver their opponents.

Male and female servants and many supply wagons followed the army on long marches. Records are vague as to the organization of the army, although the names and ranks of the officers are mentioned. Assyrian war records concentrated more on recording victories than with detailing the mundane life of the common soldier.

Chariots

The chariot appeared in Mesopotamia between 3000-2500 B.C. The Sumerians used heavier and larger vehicles with four wheels and a crew of four men: a driver, a warrior, and two shield bearers. The warrior carried javelins and spears. King Solomon's forces included hundreds of chariots, archers, spears, javelins, and slingers.

Early Weapons

When David fought with Goliath, he described the Philistine's weapons: "You come to me with a sword and with a spear and with a javelin . . ."

(1 Samuel 17:45 RSV). For personal combat, these were perhaps the most powerful weapons of his day.

The spears and javelins used by the Israelites when they entered Canaan had wooden shafts and metal points. Warriors used the spear for thrusting, while the smaller, lighter-weight javelin could also be thrown.

Early swords were generally short, straight, double edged, and used for stabbing in hand-to-hand combat. Judges 3:16 (TLB) describes Ehud's dagger: "Before he went on this journey he made himself a double-edged dagger eighteen inches long and hid it in his clothing, strapped against his right thigh."

During the Israelite conquest of the Promised Land, a sickle-shaped sword became common, for it could be easily swung from the chariot. But by the time David fought Goliath, the long sword, introduced to the area by the Sea Peoples, would have been in the Philistines' hands.

On the other hand, when he attacked the Philistine hero, David used a sling, something a shepherd might use against marauding wolves. The Bible expresses the surprise of David's victory over the well-armed giant:

Reaching into his bag and taking out a stone, he slung it and struck the Philistine on the forehead. The stone sank into his forehead, and he fell facedown on the ground. So David triumphed over the Philistine with a sling and a stone; without a sword in his hand he struck down the Philistine and killed him (I Samuel 17:49, 50 NIV).

SLINGS

The first projectile weapon was a simple, hand-thrown rock. This was improved by a rock with a string attached. The thrower swung the rock by its string repeatedly to build up speed, and then he threw the string along with the rock. This weapon evolved to allow the rock to separate from the cord by use of a pouch. The range of a basic sling was about 100 yards. The sling was either twirled underhand for long distance or overhand for short distances.

The sling consisted of a small patch of leather with two cords attached to the opposite edges. A stone was placed on the patch and the strings pulled, so the patch formed a small bag for the stone. The warrior swung this around his head several times, building velocity. At the proper moment, he would release one cord, causing the stone to fly out at the same velocity along a tangent of its circular path. The terminal velocity of the twirling stone in the sling was equal to the initial velocity of the stone in flight. From that point on, air resistance slowed the projectile as it dropped back to the ground. The slung stone achieved a far greater speed than one thrown by hand (Reader's Digest Editors *People* 1981, 41, 166)

A phalanx of soldiers throwing stones at an approaching enemy was demoralizing, if not lethal. The sling eventually became a valuable battlefield weapon, since it gave a soldier a long-range threat on any terrain. This weapon was easy to make, and ammunition was plentiful. But consistently hitting one's target required a great deal of training and practice.

ARCHERY

The next great advance in weaponry—the bow and arrow—was probably the first weapon designed to concentrate energy. Most bows were made of an elastic wood or brass. The surface of the bow farthest from the string was called the back; the inner surface was the belly. The center, where the archer held the bow, was the grip, and the parts on either side of the grip were the arms or limbs. Bowstrings were made from the intestines of oxen or camels and were attached to the ends of the arms.

The arrow had three parts; each made of a different material to suit its function. The arrowhead was flint, bone, or metal, the hardest available material. The body, or shaft, was of reed or a lightweight wood. This needed to be long, thin, hard, and strong, to direct the energy transmitted from the string on release. The tail, usually made of feathers, kept the arrow on course in a smooth and straight flight.

The archer placed the base of the arrow against the string and pulled the string as far as possible from the wood, creating maximum tension. This placed the bow under a bending stress, with tension on the back and compression on the belly. Since the wood had a high modulus of elasticity or rigidity, it conserved most of the energy expended in drawing the string back. When the archer suddenly released the string, the conserved

Fig. 142. Shapes of ancient bows

From the simple curved and triangular bows (left), ancient warriors developed the single convex and double convex shapes (right), attempting to gain the greatest amount of tension while still maintaining a manageable size.

(or potential) energy in the bow was also released. The bow returned almost instantly to its original shape, and the string propelled the arrow forward with great force and speed. The stabilizing effect of the heavy arrowhead and light tail feathers kept the arrow on course.

Some bows had an effective range of 300 to 400 yards, though an arrow could go twice as far with lower accuracy. A good archer could shoot ten to fifteen arrows a minute. The crossbow, though smaller and easier to carry, lacked the range of the conventional bow and could fire only about two arrows per minute.

A bow's range depended on its size and shape, the pliability and toughness of the wood, and the archer's strength. The bigger the bow, the more energy it could store—and thus it could propel arrows farther. Yet large bows could be difficult to carry and operate.

Through time, warriors experimented with different shapes and materials for bows, trying to maximize the bow's tension without necessarily increasing its length. From the simple curved and triangular bows developed the single concave and double concave styles (see Figure 142). At first, bows were fashioned from a single piece of wood. Later "composite" bows had several thin pieces of wood glued together; some had sections of bone in the belly.

During Hammurabi's time (1792-1750 B.C.) the bow and arrow was the main weapon of choice. The geometric shape and elastic properties of the bow's limbs classified the bow. The shape would have defined each bow as a *working-recurve* or a *non-recurve*. The latter was used in Egypt and Assyria, called the *angular bow,* in which the string and the bow formed a triangular shape.

Of course, the archer needed a quiver to hold his arrows. Made of a lightweight material, the quiver typically held twenty to thirty arrows and was carried on the back or over the shoulder, so the archer could keep both hands free.

Fig. 143. Ancient tail feathers and arrowheads

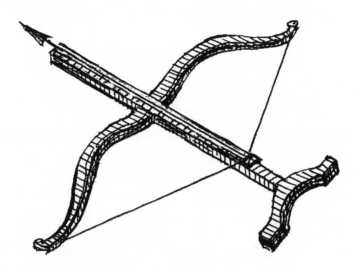

Fig. 144. Belly weapon or Heron's gastraphete

This early crossbow consisted of horn and had a curved crosspiece at the butt end for bracing against the chest or stomach while arming (hence its name). The main wood strut between the bow and the butt ends contained a track, bronze rack (or batten), pawns, and a slide that held the dart or arrow (Ferrill, 1985, 171).

Fig. 145. Loading a crossbow

According to Hero, this weapon was similar to the crossbow. It was called the "belly-shooter" (in Greek, gastrophetes) because it had to be loaded by the belly. It dates before the fourth century B.C. The archer used both arms to pull back on the bow, leaned against the curved back, placed the head against the ground, and drove the slider back.

Fig. 146.
An Israelite archer

The bow and arrow required both strength and skill, but it substantially increased an army's range of attack. Not surprisingly, the Bible uses the bow as a symbol of strength. In Hannah's song, the Lord reigns, and *"the bows of the warriors are broken . . ."* (1 Samuel 2:4 NIV).

ARMOR
Early warriors wore helmets and body armor and carried shields for protection. Archers generally were equipped with smaller shields, if any, while spearmen and swordsman used large shields that protected most of their bodies.

Fig. 147. Roman soldier's
breastplate

Early helmets, made of brass, were mainly reserved for officers, nobles, and the more important warriors. Some warriors also wore long coats of mail, extending to the knees or ankles, while common soldiers generally wore only leather jerking, protecting their upper bodies. The Bible also mentions brass *greaves*, which protected the legs (1 Samuel 17:4-7).

Fig. 148. Roman cavalrymen

Fig. 149. Babylonian cavalryman

Fig. 150. Ancient warriors

Biblical soldiers, from left to right, include: Assyrian, Babylonian, Persian, Judean, and Roman (Reader's Digest Editors People *1981, 13, 15, 97; Reader's Digest Editors* Atlas *1981, 3, 5, 15).*

In 721 B.C., the Assyrians defeated the Northern Kingdom of Israel, Samaria, Judah, and Lachish. Only Jerusalem endured. They remained until the Persians defeated them. Cyrus seized the throne of Persia in the fifth century (559-529) and went on to conquer Egypt and Assyria. After conquering Jerusalem from the Assyrians, Cyrus permitted the Jews to pray to their own God.

Fig. 151. Headgear of an Assyrian soldier

Fig. 152. Assyrian King Sennacherib with helmet and armor

Armor scales with fastenings and lacings protected the upper body.

Fig. 153.
A Canaanite warrior

Fig. 154.
Headgear of a
Philistine warrior

Fig. 155.
Helmet of a Roman soldier

Fig. 156.
Headgear of a Roman legionnaire

**Fig. 157. Full battle gear of a
Roman infantryman**

*(Cornfeld 1981, 45, 179). Josephus
described the infantryman's equipment
as follows: "The infantry was armed
with a coat of mail and a helmet, and
carried a sword at each side; that on the
left side is by far longer of the two, the
dagger being no longer than a span in
length. The general's bodyguard of picked
infantry carry a javelin and long shield,
together with a saw, basket, ax and pick, as
well as a strap, a chain and three days'
ration so that an infantryman is about as
heavily loaded as a pack mule" (Reader's
Digest Editors Atlas 1981, 17).*

Fig. 158. Fully equipped Roman trooper
The spear and short sword were held on the right side. For personal protection the soldier wore a crested helmet, leather breastplate, and greaves (Reader's Digest Editors Atlas *1981, 17).*

Fortresses

Two major factors determined the sites of fortresses in ancient time—strategic position and water sources. These factors often conflicted with each other. Hilltop sites were easier to defend, but water sources usually lay in the valleys. Thus many fortresses were built on hills near well-watered valleys, with the fortress walls enclosing a valley water source. On occasion, a deep cistern or pit would be dug inside the walls and connected by a tunnel to the stream or spring outside the walls. This was Hezekiah's solution to Jerusalem's water problem (2 Kings 20:20).

Walls served both defensive and offensive functions. Obviously, they prevented enemy troops from overrunning a fortress, but walls also gave defenders a position from which to attack the enemy. The Bible describes the war preparations of King Uzziah of Judah (791-739 B.C.): ". . . in Jerusalem he made machines designed by skillful men for use on the towers and on the corner defenses to shoot arrows and hurl large stones . . . " (2 Chronicles 26:15 NIV).

Walls needed to be thick and high to prevent battering and scaling—and deep enough to keep the enemy from tunneling under them. They also required the strength to withstand catapulted rocks. Moats dug around the walls helped keep attackers away. Sloping walls, or *glacis*, deflected battering rams' impact and enabled defenders to roll large rocks down upon an onrushing enemy. The top of the wall gave defenders a good vantage point to see the attackers and to fire on them. Fortress wall design could leave no dead spots, or concealed corners that an enemy might scale unobserved. Thus many fortresses had irregularly shaped walls, crenellated parapets, special towers, and bastions for the defending archers and spearmen.

The gate of a fortress was its most vulnerable part. It needed to give friends access and deny entrance to foes. Thus ancient military engineers designed gates carefully, usually placing them at the steepest part of the hill. An access road had to wind back and forth, maintaining a practical slope for those ascending, but keeping unwanted enemies from rushing the gate. Where possible, the road reached the gate with the fortress on the right side. This exposed the attacker's right side to fire from the wall. Since a warrior general held his shield on his left arm, the attacking soldier was especially vulnerable on his right.

In some cases, two carefully situated gates protected a city or fortress. If attackers managed to penetrate the outer gate, they would have to approach the main gate with their right sides exposed.

Doors at these entryways were generally made of metal-clad wood, to keep attackers from setting them afire. Their openings had to be wide enough accommodate chariots and wagons; so two swinging doors typically covered the space, meeting at the center. A heavy beam, lying across the doors and set recessed sockets of the stone walls, locked the doors. Sometimes the sockets were lined with bronze to reduce wear and tear.

Towers on either side also protected the gate. From these vantage points, defenders could fire arrows and spears or pour burning oil on anyone attempting to ram the doors or smash their hinges. Some fortresses even had a roof with holes constructed over the gate area, which allowed the defending soldiers to fire downward, directly upon the attackers' heads. In essence, there were often sub-fortresses built around a fortress gate, since that was generally the structure's most vulnerable point (Ussishkin 1988, 42-47).

THE FORTRESS AT JERICHO

Dating to the Middle Bronze period (about 2000 B.C.), this fortification included a glacis of beaten earth with a brick wall at the top. Over time, two more glacis were added on top of the first one. The last of these, a stone embankment, was built about 1750 B.C. and destroyed about 1550 B.C. (Paul 1973, 84, 85). (See figure 112 for a typical glacis and moat.)

Fig. 159. Through section of an ancient protective stone wall
To start, the builders needed solid ground upon which they could place a stone foundation. On top of this, they could begin building a wall (right) made of stone masonry and measuring nine feet high by four feet thick. Next they covered the outer face of the wall with small stones and mortar. To finish it, they packed a layer of earth on top of the mortar and in turn covered that with a sixteen-inch-thick layer of pebbles and mortar (Mazar 1975, 153).

Fig. 160. A defensive wall with glacis and moat

To discourage attacks from tunneling or using siege machines, the builders of this more sophisticated wall erected a glacis and excavated a moat that allowed defenders to counteract enemies with large stones, which were rolled down at attacking troops. The builders began by cutting a bench into the side of the hill. On top of a rubble foundation, they built a vertical wall of cut stone. To form the glacis, they sloped the front of the wall and built it up with alternate layers of beaten earth and stones. Beneath the slope, they excavated a moat.

SAUL'S FORTRESS-PALACE

The double wall and broad towers of Saul's fortress-palace at Gibeah made it the strongest Israelite citadel of its time. The space between the inner and outer walls was partitioned into chambers and used for storage. But this space could also be packed with rubble to make one solid wall, thwarting battering-ram attacks. Crenellated parapets gave defenders narrow gaps through which archers could fire arrows, while providing ample protection from the missiles of the enemy.

SOLOMON'S FORTRESS AT MEGIDDO

Megiddo lay at a crucial crossroads, where the Jezreel Valley met the famed Via Maris. Numerous armies have marched through the mountain passes in that area.

Such a strategic location demanded a solid defense, and King Solomon provided it. The city gates boasted a brilliant design. Guard towers looked down on the city's entryway, which could only be reached by a steep stairway or an exposed ramp. The outer gates had two pairs of heavy wooden doors, which opened into a courtyard enclosed by high walls. This courtyard led to the main gate, which had four sets of heavy doors. Between these were small spaces, where soldiers could be posted to surprise intruders.

FORTRESSES OF DAVID AND SOLOMON AT TAANACH

Earlier structures of brick and stone had fallen at Taanach, a few miles south of Megiddo, but Solomon used some of those materials to build a network of garrison forts. The west fort, sixty-two feet by seventy feet, was built with large boulders (cyclopean masonry). The walls, four feet thick, rested on a foundation that went down thirteen feet. A thick layer of lime and plaster coated the floor. The fort included nine or ten chambers, most likely used for storage. Archaeologists surmise that the structure was intended merely as a framework for a more impressive building or fighting platform to be built on top.

The northeast tower was built of limestone, finely dressed, squared off, and laid in regular courses. It included openings through which defenders could shoot (Reader's Digest Editors *People* 1981, 201).

HEROD'S FORTRESS AT MASADA

Herod had a way of building fortresses on the most inaccessible sites. A prime example was Masada, on a steep mountain on the west shore of the Dead Sea. When the Romans invaded Israel to put down the Jewish rebellion of A.D. 67-70, they found Masada the hardest to conquer. They besieged the fortress, but the mountaintop was self-sufficient with food and water. Eventually the Romans built a circumvallation, or siege wall, around the mountain. After two years, they finally worked their way to the top—only to find that the Jewish defenders had committed suicide rather than be captured.

Machines of War

Well-built fortresses gave defenders the advantage. The man at the top of the wall could shoot an arrow, throw a javelin, drop a boulder, or pour burning oil or molten lead on an attacker. Thus, attacking armies needed countermeasures—siege machines or war engines—that could success-fully overcome the defenders' advantage. This meant employment for military engineers, specialists who designed, built, and operated such machines.

Often engineers had to improvise. Generally, ancient armies did not carry bulky catapults with them—they would slow them down. Instead, the engineers packed the skeins, slings, and metal fittings they needed and pulled together the other materials near the battlefield. As an army pre-pared to besiege a city, soldiers cut down trees in the area and built their war machines there (Cornfeld 1981, 373).

The battering ram, depicted on reliefs of the Assyrian king Ashurnasirpal (883-859 B.C.), was one of the earliest war machines. At first just a large wooden beam carried by soldiers, it developed into a ver-itable combination of the modern tank and bulldozer. Engineers devel-oped a protective housing for the beam. This wooden frame, sometimes mounted on wheels, might have had rectangular wicket shields on the sides and a domed metal turret on top. Inside the turret, ropes held the bat-tering ram in place. The entire machine might have been five meters long and about eight meters high. Eventually, military engineers fixed an ax-like blade or metal point on the front of the ram. This device, often called a bore or pike, would be driven into joints between the stones of a wall. Once the blade or point went deep enough, it could be moved from side to side, loosening the stones and collapsing the wall. When attacking the gates of a fortress, pikes, swords, and spears were used to pry the gates loose, tearing out the hinges. Of course, this all had to be done with shields or some sort of protective structure overhead.

The prophet Ezekiel foretold the use of battering rams and other war machines in the Babylonian conquest of Jerusalem:

"The king of Babylon . . . is to set up battering rams, to give the command to slaughter, to sound the battle cry, to set battering rams against the gates, to build a ramp and to erect siege works" (Ezekiel 21:21, 22 NIV).

Classic writings tell of the Phoenician engineers who introduced a battering ram suspended by chains from the roof of a wheeled shed. This was called a ram tortoise.

Fig. 161. Battering ram

Assyrian military engineers excelled in siege warfare. One of their methods used the weight of a fortress wall against itself. Workers, or sappers, dug a hole under a wall, temporarily shoring it up with wooden supports. But then they set fire to the wood, and the wall, left unsupported, collapsed.

Though not exactly a machine, one method used by the Syrians against the Maccabees in the second century B.C. is strangely akin to the modern tank. They built wooden towers on the backs of elephants—thirty-two of them—gave the animals wine, and irked them into charging the enemy. Eleazar, brother of Judas Maccabeus, killed the largest elephant, but Eleazar died when the animal fell on him (I Maccabees 6:28-47, Apocrypha).

THE CATAPULT

The earliest catapults shot large arrows measuring up to six feet long. These machines were essentially massive crossbows mounted on pedestals.

Fig. 162. Ancient Egyptian sappers
This painting, found on a tomb wall, shows three Egyptian combat engineers in a portable hut. A reed and basketwork frame covered with hide protected sappers, who dislodged the stones from a fortress wall (Yadin 1963, 17).

Fig. 163. Ancient Assyrian battering ram and archers

Military engineers developed a rather sophisticated catapulting mechanism for cocking and releasing these huge bows. A wooden beam (the *syrinx,* or trough) was mounted on the pedestal at an angle. This had a large groove in its upper surface. The crosspiece of the bow was positioned at the top of the trough and fastened by brackets. Within the groove of the trough beam, a smaller beam (the *diostra,* projector, or slide) moved back and forth. This had a narrow groove in its upper surface and a piece of metal, or trigger, at the lower end. It had a hook to engage the bowstring and some kind of knob, handle, or lanyard to release it.

A windlass at the lower end of the trough pulled the slide piece down the groove of the trough, stretching the bowstring to the desired point. The metal trigger on the slide also had two pawls (or dogs), which clicked over the teeth of two bronze racks that ran the length of the trough's groove. These kept the slide from slipping back during the winding of the windlass.

When the bowstring was stretched tight enough (depending on the desired distance of the shot), the windlass was stopped; the teeth held the slide (and bowstring) in place, and a dart was loaded into the slide's narrow groove. By means of the trigger mechanism, the bowstring disengaged from the hook and snapped forward, sending the dart on its destructive journey. Then the slide was pulled up the trough, by hand or windlass, to engage the bowstring again (Ferrill 1985, 75, Yadin 1963, 18).

Fig. 164. Ancient Babylonian combat engine

The dart-throwing catapult more than doubled the effective range of an army. The most powerful longbows might accurately shoot 300 to 400 yards, but the catapult was effective at 600 to 800 yards (Landels 1978, 99).

Later engineers—possibly the Phoenicians—developed the stone-throwing catapult, attaching a pouch or strap in the middle of the bow-string to hold the stone. History first mentions this weapon in connection with Alexander's siege of Tyre (332 B.C.). Its range depended on the weight of the projectile (10 to 180 pounds). A 60-pound stone might fly 200 yards. The dart throwers' greater range made them more effective against enemy soldiers, but the force of the stone throwers' heavy missiles made them more effective against structures, such as ships or siege tow-ers. One problem with the stone thrower was that attacks also provided arms for the enemy. If they had catapults, they could fling the opposi-tion's own stones right back. Some armies began catapulting bricks, which usually broke on impact, so they could not be fired in return.

Enhancing the catapult's effectiveness, a torsion device used a braided rope of horsehair or human hair for tension, rather than a wooden bow. A massive frame surrounded the trough, and the rope was threaded through the sides of this frame until two strong skeins were built up. A pair of rigid throwing arms, thrust through these skeins, took the place of the arms of a solid bow.

The torsion catapult stored more energy than the flexion catapult and thus could throw heavier missiles and throw them farther. Yet it also proved harder to manage. The skeins would go slack in wet weather or with long use, and they needed regular tightening.

The *ballistae* and some other forms of the catapult used a skein of animal tendons to store and release energy. The energy stored in thirty-six pounds of tendons could throw a ninety-pound missile 400 meters. Modern-day engineers estimate that it would take 700 pounds of steel spring to match this.

Tendons became the material of choice in Roman catapults. Though some writers allowed that human hair might be substituted, the military writer Vegetius insisted, ". . . ballistae are no use unless powered by sinew-rope." Yet despite the amazing amount of energy that could be stored by tendon material, those ancient weapons were limited by the fact that the artilleryman had to crank in all the energy by hand to pull the material taut (Vogel 1986, 68).

The onager siege machine, another development in the catapult, had a single arm connected by a torsion skein. When stretched and released, the skein propelled the arm in a vertical plane against a padded stop. At the end of the arm, a sling or spoon held the projectile. (See Figure 116.)

A sturdy, bolted frame held a heavy, padded stop that halted the arc of the wooden throwing arm. A torsion skein of rope or women's hair would conserve the energy provided by a soldier, who manually turned the winch or windlass behind the arm.

From the wooden arm hung the sling that held the ballista stone. By turning the winch, the soldier pulled the arm back, tightening the skein so he could fit the stone into the sling. With a trigger mechanism, he released the stored energy in the skein, sending the arm swinging rapidly against the stop and throwing the stone forward.

Because this machine could throw such enormous projectiles, defenders could crush men, horses, and enemy machines that came before their walls. Naming it an onager, after the wild ass, reflected the catapult's kick. As Vitruvius described its use:

"The catapult operated the same way as the later cross-bow. The pair of vertical coil chambers was at the front, the bow being drawn back by a windlass to the required limit of tension. The bow was released by a trigger and the bolt shot along a trough with an aperture at the front" (Mazar 1975, 90).

The onager gave way to the trebuchet, or counterweight catapult, an enormous sling placed at the end of a jib, which carried a counterweight at its other end. The jib pivoted on two pins, and a large stand supported

Fig. 165. An onager catapult

A war machine that worked particularly effectively against oncoming armies was the onager catapult, or one-armed torsion stone thrower.

Missile

1-Loaded

2-Released

Missile

3-Missile in Flight

Fig. 166. Catapult in action

This figure shows the sequence of loading and firing a catapult. (1) Throwing arm is pulled back. Tightening the splein, then missile is placed in cup. (2) Throwing arm released and swings in an arc to the backstop. (3) Throwing arm stops but missile continues in flight.

the whole device. Since the jib was vertical and the counterweight very heavy, lowering the jib or raising the counterweight took great effort. Therefore the engineers constructed springs consisting of pieces of flexible wood and assembled in a T shape to ease the load. A cable with return pulleys and a turning device, which led to the end of a strong bar fixed to a winch, stretched the springs. When they were taut or the bar turned back, it required a counterweight of 1,300 cubic feet of earth to hold the machine steady.

Because it did not rely on the tension of a skein, the trebuchet worked well even in wet weather. By varying the size of the counterweight and its distance from the fulcrum, engineers could adjust the weapon's range. Some simple forms of the trebuchet used the force of soldiers pulling on ropes to propel the missile (Morgan 1960, 285).

Fig. 167. Catapult
Catapult on solid wood wheels.

Fig. 168. Catapult

A catapult ready to be fired.

Fig. 169. A torsion dart thrower

Also known as quick firers or scorpions, these catapults were generally mounted on carts. Each century of a Roman legion would have one, and it would be manned by two soldiers, turning the windlass and loading the darts. The weapon could fire a barrage of spears about 300 meters.

NAVAL ARTILLERY

The machinery of warfare developed on sea as well as on land. In 313 B.C., Demetrius, who had worked with siege engines on land, put catapults and ballistae on galley ships. With dart-throwing catapults on the prow, his vessels could launch preliminary barrages against enemy craft long before they came within bowshot. Through time, naval catapults used larger and heavier ammunition, such as stones, which could do considerable damage to enemy ships, and *"Greek fire,"* stones, which were covered with cloth soaked in naphtha, crude oil, sulfur, and pitch (Ferrill 1985, 85).

Fig. 170. A shipboard catapult
(Mansir 1981, 46).

Fire proved to be a crucial weapon in naval combat. In the second century B.C., the Rhodians won sea battles by hanging pots with Greek fire in front of their galleys.

Later warriors learned that saltpeter, added to the Greek-fire recipe, caused spontaneous combustion. This led to two more types of incendiary weapons. One was a catapult that tossed clay jars filled with a self-igniting mixture. These jars broke on impact, creating an explosion. The other weapon was actually a rocket launcher. A reed was filled with the Greek-fire mixture, capped with a stopper, and placed in a bronze tube on deck. The tube was aimed and a fuse lit. When the reed ignited, it released gases that propelled it out of the tube and in a flaming streak toward the target. In close combat between vessels, the Greeks used another form of this weapon. A large tube of wood lined with bronze was set on the fore-deck and connected to an air pump. The tube was filled with Greek fire, then lit. As the sailors worked the pump, a shaft of flame shot outward, as in a modern flamethrower.

Pericles used a similar weapon in land warfare at Samos in about 441 B.C., when he commanded his soldiers to set fire to wooden stockade walls:

> They . . . hollowed out a great beam . . . and suspended a vessel by chains at the end of the beam; the iron mouth of the bellows directed down-wards into the vessel attached to the beam, of which a great part was itself overlaid with iron. The machine they brought up from a distance on carts to various points of the rampart . . . and when it was quite near the wall they applied a large bellows to their own end of the beam, and blew through it, the blast, prevented from escaping, passed into the vessel which contained burning coals and sulfur and pitch; these made a huge flame, and set fire to the rampart, so that no one could remain upon it (De Camp 1963, 101).

In Roman conflicts of 38 B.C., Agrippa used a variation of the dart-throwing catapult in his battles against the lighter and faster ships of Sextus. His catapult shot an iron rod, tipped with a grapnel, and attached to a line. Shot at an enemy ship, it would sink into the vessel, and sailors could pull the line, bringing the two ships close together. Agrippa's troops could then board the enemy ships and defeat them in hand-to-hand com-bat. The catapult gave Agrippa much greater range than the hand-thrown grapnel, a necessity against the swift craft of Sextus.

HOW THESE MACHINES WORKED

Each of these machines of war worked according to certain properties of physics, making use of predictable scientific laws. The engineer merely harnessed them to achieve his goals.

The battering ram simply used the weight of the massive beam against the wall or structure being assaulted. When it swung, the kinetic energy of the moving ram converted suddenly into explosive energy, shattering the stone of the wall. By increasing the ram's weight and lengthening the ropes suspending the ram, engineers could provide the swinging ram with greater kinetic energy. They could increase this by providing additional manpower behind the ram.

The catapult used the potential energy stored in the stretched skein. When released, the skein transferred this energy to the arm, which swung upward in an arc until stopped suddenly by the heavy frame. The projectile—the stone or arrow being thrown—continued in a direction tangential to the arc of the arm's movement. Its initial velocity would equal the speed of the arm just before it stopped. This velocity depended on the degree of tension in the rope and how far the arm had to move before being stopped by the frame.

Ancient military engineers learned to adjust the projectile's direction and speed (and therefore its range) by setting the catapult at different angles and winding the windlass more or less. They had to be aware of the laws governing the act of sending the missile into the air, as well as the laws of gravity, which pulled the missile back to earth and to its target.

The initial velocity of the missile can be divided into vertical and horizontal components. Simply take the vertical velocity and subtract the acceleration due to gravity—this will determine the time of flight. This would be similar to shooting an object straight up and seeing how long it took to fall back to earth—at some point the downward pull of gravity will overcome the upward power of the initial shot, and the missile will fall. Then, when the time of flight is determined, one can figure from the horizontal velocity just how far the missile will go across the terrain in that time.

Catapult operators had two main variables as they aimed their weapons: the angle of the throwing arm at impact and the amount of tension in the skein. Once they knew the speed at which a specific number of turns on the windlass would propel a stone of a certain weight, their calculation of the angle gave them a good idea of where the stone would fall. To increase that velocity, they tightened the skein more. To change the relation between vertical velocity and horizontal velocity, they changed the angle. In modern artillery calculations, air resistance and other factors are also considered, but ancient artillerymen probably compensated for these factors by trial and error.

Fig. 171. A grappling catapult

The Romans mounted this offensive weapon, consisting of a pedestal, bow, bowstring, and iron grappling dart, on the gunwales of their men-of-war. When the soldier cut the line that held the bow taut, the dart shot across to the deck of the enemy ship and lodged there. The attackers used the rope attached near the dart's head to pull the craft close for boarding (Mansir 1981, 47).

The Roman Assault on Jerusalem

One of the best examples of the use of military engineering in ancient warfare comes from Jewish history: the Roman conquest of Jerusalem in A.D. 70.

The Jews had been under Roman rule since 64 B.C. Although they prospered economically during this time, the Jews chafed under the insensitive treatment of puppet kings like the Herods and later governors like Pontius Pilate. In A.D. 43, Emperor Caligula even tried to install a statue of himself in the Jerusalem Temple.

The spark of rebellion came in A.D. 66, when the Greek population of Caesarea turned on the Jews who lived there. Josephus says they slaughtered 20,000 Jews in one hour. The Roman garrison stationed in Caesarea did nothing to stop the bloodbath.

The Jews of Jerusalem retaliated with a successful attack on the Roman garrison in their city. Then the Roman governor of Syria marched toward Jerusalem with the Twelfth Roman legion to put down the uprising. But the Jews ambushed this army in a narrow pass at Beth-horon. Soundly defeated in the battles of the day, the Romans beat a hasty retreat at night, leaving behind their heavy equipment, including catapults and slings.

The thrill of victory did not last long for the Jewish rebels, as Rome's massive army mobilized to quash the revolt. Throughout the empire,

Fig. 172. Catapult trajectory

To figure the most effective way to hit his target, the ancient artilleryman had to know the physics behind his machine. When the catapult's throwing arm hit the stop, the projectile flew upward, continuing the arc the swinging arm had begun. The stone continued at the velocity at which it had begun until the force of gravity pulled it down, sending it in a parabolic curve. As it descended it struck the ground or target. To adjust the missile's flight, the engineer adjusted the skein that provided the energy or alter the place at which the arm hit the stop.

thirty legions (of about 5,000 men each) were alerted. Ten legions were stationed within a two-month march of Jerusalem. They came with their war machines: the swinging rams, the catapults, and the rapid-fire dart throwers. By contrast, the Jews relied on guerrilla warfare: hand-to-hand combat and a thorough knowledge of their rocky terrain.

By A.D. 70, General Vespasian, conqueror of Britain, had bottled up the rebels in Jerusalem. He returned in glory to Rome, where he was named emperor, leaving the siege of Jerusalem to his son, Titus.

The Tenth Legion approached Jerusalem and set up camp on the Mount of Olives, which overlooked the city from the east. The Jews attacked this encampment and were rebuffed by Roman reinforcements. In response, Titus cleared the gardens just outside the walls—to prevent any more sneak attacks—and set up his assault force on the northwest side of the city.

About 150 yards northwest of what is now Jaffa Gate, the Romans began assaulting the wall of the city with three battering rams. They also wheeled three assault towers into place adjacent to the walls. These towered over the walls, enabling Roman archers to fire on any Jewish defenders who might try to fire down upon those operating the rams. In addition, the ram force was protected with wooden shields covered with hides, to deflect flaming arrows and burning oil. Roman archers, bolt firers, and stingers also maintained a steady barrage at the parapets and any openings in the wall. Further back, Roman slings and catapults added to the assault.

Finally the rams broke through the wall, and the Romans entered, forcing the Jews to retreat to the second wall. The Romans then began to assault the wall southwest of what is now the Damascus Gate. Five days of battering broke this wall, too, and 1,500 legionnaires moved into the Jerusalem marketplace.

Suddenly, the soldiers found themselves in the winding alleys of an unfamiliar city. This was the Jews turf, and one-to-one combat on the narrow streets worked to their advantage. The Romans had to pull back again.

The Jews quickly rebuilt the wall, but in five days the Romans had broken through again. This time, the soldiers burned the marketplace and forced the defenders behind their inner wall. The Romans sent legions to attack the Upper City and the Antonia Fortress, while their engineers built a huge assault tower.

Fig. 173. Siege machines in action

Military engineers use three types of catapults (or ballistae) to attack a walled city. In the foreground two soldiers winch down the throwing arm of a catapult while others prepare the 180-pound balls for firing. In the background a testudo (or tortoise) is readied for attack. At the right, soldiers hide behind an armed approach shield (Yadin 1963, 16-24, 314, 437; Rabinovich 1971, 50-55; De Camp 1963, 181).

Fig. 174. An assault on a fortress

As defenders shoot their bows and arrows and lose spears against them, the attacking soldiers make use of a wheeled siege tower covered in the front with rawhides and fitted with a gangplank (at top) and a battering ram (at the base). Meanwhile, to each side, more soldiers climb a scaling ladder that reaches the top of the wall (Cornfeld 1982, 39, 231).

But the Romans were not the only ones using military engineering. The Jews had about 150 catapults and other war engines, captured from the twelfth legion four years earlier. They had trained themselves to operate these, and they bombarded the attackers with some success. They also employed an ingenious plan to build tunnels under the areas where the Romans would place their assault towers. As they dug, they shored up the tunnel with wood struts covered with pitch. Then they filled the shaft with combustible material. When the Romans rolled their heavy towers up to the wall, the Jews set fire to the tunnel, burning the wooden struts. The ground gave way, and the assault towers toppled.

Realizing the strategic importance of Roman machines and towers, the Jews launched a series of forays against those weapons themselves. Because the Romans were running out of building materials for new machines, they had to go farther and farther for timber. But in essence, the Jews just bought time. The Romans were the most powerful army the world had known, and they kept battering away at the walls.

Eventually, the wall over the tunnels collapsed. The Romans streamed in, engaging the defenders in hand-to-hand combat. After about a month, the Romans broke into the Temple area. Josephus says General Titus wanted to spare the Temple, but his soldiers ran out of control. They burned the Temple and eventually pushed its rubble over the eastern retaining wall.

11

Water Supply

PEOPLE NEED WATER FOR DRINKING, WASHING, IRRIGATING, AND cooking. Societies have always depended on their springs, wells, lakes, or rivers. In ancient times, cities grew around water sources. But as cities expanded, they needed better water management. Greater population meant greater demand for water—and potentially greater pollution of the water supply. The health—and sometimes survival—of the society was at stake.

Great civilizations learned to manage their water well. They developed cisterns, aqueducts, and piping systems for the inflow of fresh water and the disposal of waste.

Approximately 5,500 years ago, in Egypt, palace apartments had copper water pipes. The designers of the Great Pyramid also installed copper piping for the royal bathing pool of Pharaoh Cheops. To the northeast, the Babylonians dug a network of canals connected to large underground drainage sewers made of brick. In the eastern Mediterranean, homes in Crete had bathtubs and toilets made of hard pottery, dating to about 1,000 B.C.

The Romans are often credited with the invention of hydraulic engineering, but even they borrowed from their Etruscan predecessors.

Rome's Cloaca Maxima, which still carries water to the Tiber River, was built by an Etruscan king in about 400 B.C.

Yet the Romans did bring the art of sanitation to a higher level, building massive aqueducts, extensive underground sewer systems, and public and private baths. They used lead and bronze piping and marble fixtures with fittings of gold and silver. Much of this was plundered when the Vandals and Goths invaded Rome. Succeeding centuries saw a great neglect of water management, resulting in widespread disease.

Water Conduits

Many Mediterranean countries used pipes to conduct water. Much of this piping was made from lead, which was plentiful in Spanish mines. (Vitruvius was one of the first to warn of this metal's health hazards.)

In the foundations and retaining walls of Jerusalem, one can still see the hollowed stone blocks that ancient people used as piping. These blocks were squared, hollowed out, and grooved to fit together. The resulting pipes were laid out on the ground, transporting water to homes and fields throughout the Judean hills. These were examples of the present day "bell and spigot" clay pipe.

Cisterns

The inhabitants of Jerusalem dug cisterns for water storage as early as 2000 B.C. The limestone of this region suited that purpose well—coated with lime plaster, it held water very effectively. In some cases, houses were built from the stone excavated during cistern construction.

Many such household reservoirs still exist in Jerusalem's rocky ground. Cut sixteen to twenty-three feet deep, they are generally bottle shaped. That is, the base is a cube or cylinder with vertical walls, but it narrows near the top to an opening about three feet in diameter. Many cisterns include depressions in the bottom to catch mud and sand sediment, so that a jar lowered into the cistern will bring back only clear water.

The Bible indicates that cisterns were already built in Palestine before the Israelites settled there. The Lord told them that the Promised Land

included "houses full of all good things, which you did not fill, and cisterns hewn out, which you did not hew . . ." (Deuteronomy 6:11 RSV).
King Uzziah's building projects included public cisterns built in the
desert to enable herdsmen to water their animals. As part of the propa-
ganda of Assyria's threat to Jerusalem, King Sennacherib promised the
Jews: " . . . Make peace with me and come out to me. Then every one of
you will eat from his own vine and fig tree and drink water from his own
cistern" (2 Kings 18:31 NIV).

Fig. 175. A potsherd drain
*Such a drain directed water collected from a flat roof into the mouth of a cistern
(Canaan 1954, 18).*

Fig. 176. A hollowed stone pipe

Fig. 177. Roman lead pipes
During the empire, the Romans crafted pipes from lead sheets. After bending them to the proper shape, they lapped or folded the metal and soldered it closed with tin or an alloy of tin and lead (Landels 1978, 43).

The land of Israel can be very dry, but it also has regular times of rain. Thus it was essential to make the best use of rainwater when it came. For this purpose, the flat roofs of houses were plastered, curbed, and slightly sloped. Rain collected in a corner of the roof and descended through clay pipes to the cistern or a large urn. Courtyards were often paved with stone and similarly curbed and sloped so that rainwater flowed toward the underground reservoir.

Water-Supply Sites

OPHEL

The history of the settlement of Jerusalem demonstrates the importance of water supply and storage. The first inhabitants lived on Ophel, the lower eastern ridge of the city. This was quite vulnerable to attack, but it was close to the water supply—the springs in the Kidron Valley. After the development of lime mortar, about 1000 B.C., cisterns could be made quite waterproof, but the first residents of Jerusalem still used mud mortar, which allowed a great deal of seepage. Thus they had to live close to running water. After lime mortar came into use, residents depended less on the Kidron springs. They could settle the higher ridges and live off the rainwater from their watertight cisterns.

Fig. 178. Excavation of a cistern

THE TEMPLE MOUNT

Under the Temple Mount's courtyard lie at least thirty-seven reservoirs. The largest, *Bahr* ("the lake"), is 40 feet deep, 246 yards in circumference, with a capacity of 13,600 cubic yards (12,000 cubic meters). Some say the aqueduct from the Solomon Pools, near Bethlehem, supplied it.

HEZEKIAH'S TUNNEL

As Jerusalem became larger and more important, it needed a safer water supply. Under normal circumstances, the cisterns would suffice, supplemented by occasional trips to the Gihon spring outside the walls, in the Kidron Valley. But in times of siege, the city was cut off from this spring. When the Assyrians ran rampant through the Middle East, Hezekiah decided to prepare for a possible siege by digging a tunnel from the spring to a reservoir within the city walls. Using hammers and chisels, Hezekiah's workmen carved their way through 1,749 feet of solid limestone, removing some 850 cubic yards of rock. Two teams apparently worked simultaneously, one digging from the spring, the other from the reservoir. It took an estimated 200 days—and the tunnel twists and turns through the rock—but the two teams eventually met.

Fig. 179. An ancient cistern

To build this reservoir, solid rock had to be excavated, to form (1) a basin that held the water, (2) a shaft that reached the surface, and (3) a drain that carried the water to the shaft. Once the rock was removed, workers applied lime plaster to the cistern and used stone and cement to line the shaft. Finally they sealed the top of the shaft with a protective stone cap.

In 1800, a schoolboy exploring the tunnel found an inscription announcing the completion of the project. Though only the latter part of the inscription remains and parts of it are unclear, it still gives a feeling of the joy those workmen must have experienced:

[When] (the tunnel) was driven through. And this was the way in which it was cut through: While [I (were) still [I axe(s), each man toward his fellow, and while there was still three cubits to cut through, [there was heard] the voice of a man calling to his fellow, for there was an overlap in the rock at the right [and on the left]. And when the tunnel was driven through, the quarrymen hewed (the rock), each man toward his fellow, axe against axe; and the water flowed from the spring toward the reservoir for 1,200 cubits, and the height of the rock above the head(s) of the quarrymen was 100 cubits (Miller 1978, 217).

THE POOL OF GIBEON

The Bible mentions a *"pool of Gibeon,"* where the forces of David and Saul met in battle (2 Samuel 2:13). In 1956, archaeologists in Gibeon uncovered a pit thirty-seven feet in diameter, cut from solid rock, which goes down eighty-two feet, all the way to the water table. Almost 3,000 tons of limestone would have had to be removed in the process. This pool apparently served as a water source for the village of Gibeon, since a seventy-nine-step stairway, also carved from the rock, winds along its side. From the rubble found at the bottom of the pit, archaeologists determined that the pit had not been used since 6 B.C. (Reader's Digest Editors *People* 1981, 168).

WATER TUNNEL AT MEGIDDO

A similar shaft appears at Megiddo. There the problem resembled Jerusalem's: The water source, a spring, was outside the city. So in the time of Solomon, workers dug a shaft down thirty feet through the debris of previous settlements. From this rock, they built a stone wall, forming a well fifteen feet in diameter, and steps of stone leading to the bottom of the well. Then they continued digging through the rock, down to a level 120 feet below the spring. A 165-foot-long tunnel, excavated from both directions, brought the spring's water downward to the base of the well (Paul 1973, 138).

QUMRAN

The Essene community at Qumran needed water not only for the necessities of daily living, but also for their baptism rituals. Thus they built their village around a complex canal system. An aqueduct brought water into the compound, where it branched off into conduits that supplied seven major cisterns, several bathing pools, and some buildings, and then it flowed off in a waterfall to the west (Reader's Digest Editors People 1981, 303).

Greek and Roman Waterworks

Herodotus described two of the great Greek engineering feats found on the island of Sarnos:

> One is a tunnel, under a hill 900 feet high, carried entirely through the base of a hill, with a mouth at either end. The length of the cutting is almost a mile—the height and width are eight feet. Along the whole course there is a second cutting, thirty feet deep and three feet broad, whereby water is brought through pipes, from an abundant source to the city. . . . Such is the first of their great works; the second is a mole in the sea, which goes all round the harbor, nearly 120 feet deep, and in length over 400 yards (Miller 1966, 168).

Explored by archaeologists in the 1870s and 1880s, the tunnel proved to be about two-thirds the size Herodotus had recorded—3,300 feet long and five and a half feet in height and width. It had a trench for a clay pipe. Tunneling from both ends, the miners had apparently missed meeting at the middle by only twenty feet horizontally and three feet vertically.

The Romans, of course, claimed their water-supply engineering was far superior to anyone else's, and they were probably right. In the second century A.D., Trajan's water commissioner, Frontinus, announced: ". . . With such an array of indispensable structures carrying so many waters, compare, if you will, the idle pyramids or the useless, though famous, works of the Greeks" (De Camp 1963, 172).

The Romans began building their water system in 312 B.C., and the ancient world had never seen anything like it. By A.D. 226, eleven aqueducts delivered 260 million gallons of fresh water each day to the city of Rome. More than 250 miles of aqueducts brought water from sources in the hills, along the hydraulic gradient, over canyons and valleys, into the city. Pressure from the elevated aqueducts forced water through a complex network of channels and conduits that ran under the streets of Rome (Babbitt 1939, 2, 3).

In that time, aqueducts became popular public works throughout the empire. It seemed as if every governor or provincial king wanted to put a modern Roman water system in his major cities.

In 9 B.C., Herod the Great installed an aboveground aqueduct for his favorite city of Caesarea, which had a population of 40,000. This aqueduct carried fresh water from the springs of Mount Carmel, over five miles away. The structure consisted of an elevated channel lined with plaster and supported by masonry arches. In some areas, concrete covered the channel, so the flowing water could be siphoned upward for short distances by hydraulic pressure.

Fig. 180. A stone aqueduct

The ancient builders erected two parallel walls of brick or ashlar stone, which they lined with lime plaster. After filling in the lower portion with concrete or rubble, they laid a concrete floor and capped the aqueduct with flat 7-9 stones (Landels 1978, 38).

It is obvious that, even here, the Roman engineers knew principles of hydraulic flow in open channels, since they generally built the aqueduct along the hydraulic grade line.

In Libya, a 100-mile aqueduct between Jebel and Leptis Magna carried not only water, but also olive oil. Poured in at Jebel, the oil rode atop the water until it was skimmed off at Leptis Magna and placed in separate containers for export.

Fig. 181. A Roman aqueduct

In order to bring water where it was needed, the Romans built aqueducts that passed through landmasses and over low places. Here one brings water from a higher, distant reservoir to a town that lacks a local water supply. By building on a slope, the Romans made use of hydraulic pressure. The average angle in this case is one foot of height for every 200 feet of aqueduct. At right, a subterranean tunnel (specus) lies beneath vertical shafts (putei) that provided the miners with ventilation and allowed surveyors to keep construction on a straight course. At left a stone arch (arcuatio) creates a level course for the aqueduct (Landels 1978, 40).

Roman aqueduct construction required a great deal of tunneling. Early sewers and drains used a simple cut-and-cover method: dig a trench, install a masonry conduit, and backfill around it with dirt.

But in some areas, the water's flow line was too deep for the cut-and-cover method. In this case, workmen dug two shafts to the proper depth and then excavated tunnels across, connecting the two shafts by a single, deep tunnel. Tunnels were generally narrow, with room for only one workman. Here, too, they dug simultaneously from two ends. Even with the use of plumb lines, however, the two tunnels did not always align.

Fig. 182. Roman aqueduct in Spain

A beautiful example of a Roman aqueduct built in Segovia, Spain. The water channel is at the top, and arches reach a height of ninety-eight feet. This immense structure brings water from the Rio Frio to the city, a total distance of 2400 feet. Water is filtered through a series of tanks along the way.

Of course, workmen often had to dig through rock—a grueling task. Drilling and wedging, they slowly broke away the rock. Sometimes they alternately used fire and cold water to crack the rock's surface. Digging became even more difficult when workers encountered underground water. The only mechanism with which they could remove water was Archimedes' screw, but this could not work in the confines of a narrow shaft, so often the water had to be lifted out in buckets (Armytage 1961, 19).

Fig. 183. Ancient methods of moving water

To move small quantities of water, ancient man had machines that could be worked by hand. At lower right, a man operates an Archimedes' screw. Inside a wooden stave tube lays a solid spiral screw attached to a round timber shaft. The upper and lower ends of the shaft are fixed to the ground and streambed so that the entire apparatus can rotate. As the man turns the handle on top of the shaft, the water is carried upward. At the top, an Egyptian carries water from the river into an irrigation channel by using a shadoof. *Below him is a leather container, which he has filled with water. A line attaches it to the beam above him. The pillar, halfway down the beam, provides the fulcrum, and a counterweight or centerpoise, at the end of the beam, balances the weight of the water (Readers Digest Editors People 1981, 66).*

The Chain Pump

The Babylonians lifted water from the Euphrates River to an irrigation channel to irrigate the Hanging Gardens of Babylon. The system consisted of two large wheels, one above the other, connected by a chain with buckets attached to it. The lower wheel was attached to a shaft and a handle. Slaves turned the handle to provide power to the chain pump.

As the wheel was turned, the buckets dipped into the river and picked up water. The chain then lifted the buckets to the upper wheel where they were tipped, dumping the water into a collection pool. The chain then carried the empty buckets down to be refilled. Gates released water in the pool into channels that irrigated the plants

Household water was usually stored in large pottery jars, hand carried from the river by household slaves. Jars were unglazed so that evaporation cooled the water.

Sanitation and Sewerage

Healthy societies need not only a dependable water supply, but also a safe way of discharging wastewater. Thus drains and sewers also became important building projects in ancient cities.

In Jerusalem, a drainage system carried off the water used in religious rites. Other sites had extensive storm sewers. While the royal latrine at Sargon's palace in Assyria (Dur Shariukin) had a water jar and clay dipper for flushing the facilities, the palace at Knossus, Crete, had a constant-flow flushing system. Latrine drains were usually separated from other systems so that noxious gases would not rise through system inlets.

In Roman times, city planners built sewers under the streets, rather than under buildings. In Caesarea, archaeologists found a drain opening in the center of a paved street. It appears to be a ten-foot-deep manhole, leading to an arched layer of brick—a remnant of an ancient sewer system.

In fact, Josephus commented on the elaborate construction of Caesarea's sewers. Half the time spent building this new city, he said, was allocated to the sewer system. "Some of the sewers led at equal distances from one another to the harbor and the sea, while one diagonal passage connected all of them, so that rain water and refuse of the inhabitants were easily carried off" (Josephus *Jewish Antiquities* 15:340).

12

Travel and Transportation

FROM EARLY TIMES, THE LAND OF PALESTINE HAS BEEN A CROSS-roads. At the intersection of Europe, Asia, and Africa, it became the hub of ancient caravan routes between major civilizations.

The *Via Maris* began in Egypt, at Zoan, on the Nile delta, and followed the Mediterranean coast to Gaza and Megiddo. Then it continued north to Hazor and on into Syria.

The King's Highway lay just east of Palestine. Beginning at the Nile, north of Memphis at On, the King's Highway moved east to Elath, then north along the Transjordan Plateau toward Hazor and Damascus. The traveler could then continue northeast to Tadynor and east to Babylon and Ur on the Euphrates. This is the route on which Moses led the Israelites before their entry into Canaan, after he promised the Moabites and Edomites that his people would stay *"on the main road"* (Numbers 20:17 TLB). In addition, a series of east-west roads connected Mediterranean cities to Nineveh, Assur, Dumah, and other cities in the current-day nations of Iran, Iraq, and Saudi Arabia.

Thus Israel's very geography made transportation a crucial part of its national life.

Animal Power

In biblical times, various animals transported goods and carried passengers—the wild ass (onager), donkey, ox, horse, and mule. The horse had greater speed, but oxen were twice as strong and cheaper to feed. Mules and donkeys tended to be less temperamental than horses and carried loads more willingly. The rocky terrain of central Palestine also cut down the possible speed of a journey, so mules and donkeys were generally preferred for large loads and long distances (Landels 1978, 13).

Throughout the Bible, horses suggest warfare and wealth. In prosperous times, Israel could afford to mount a cavalry. Escaping from slavery in Egypt, the Israelites went on foot, while the Egyptians chased with their horses and chariots. But in the golden years of Solomon, Israel's stables were full. "Solomon had forty thousand stalls of horses for his chariots, and twelve thousand horsemen" (1 Kings 4:26 KJV). In fact, Solomon conducted extensive trade, buying chariots from Egypt and horses from Asia, for export to Hittite and Aramean kings (1 Kings 10:29).

Wheeled Vehicles

The first "wheeled" vehicle was probably "invented" when someone edged a log under a heavy block of stone being moved from a quarry. As this procedure developed, quarry workers used rows of logs—when one slipped from the back; they would place it in front. Eventually, wooden rails were placed lengthwise in the path of the heavy object, and the logs carrying stone rolled evenly.

Later, the logs were cut into wheels and attached to a wooden axle beneath a cart that transported cargo. The wheel developed from a single slice of log to sections of a log pieced together. Still later, a band of metal set around the edge of the wheel made it more durable.

The Philistines mounted a cart on a single axle with two wooden wheels. The wheels consisted of sections of wood held together with a metal strip and surrounded by a metal rim. Babylonian ruins include copper wheel rims, but most civilizations, including that of the Philistines, used iron.

The carrying capacity of those ancient carts depended largely on the wheel design. The Philistines excelled in this area. They cut three pieces from longitudinal sections of a log, split parallel to the grain. Then they fitted the two outer semicircular pieces around the inner piece, locking them together with metal straps and spikes. After heating up the metal rim, they placed it around the wheel. When it cooled, the rim shrank, locking the pieces of the wheel sturdily in place.

Though at first the Philistines used their carts merely for hauling, the neighboring Canaanites developed carts for use in battle. Egyptians and Babylonians also began to build chariots. For success in battle, these carts needed greater speed and maneuverability, which the heavy, bulky wheels did not provide. So the Babylonians began taking sections of wood out of the wheel, resulting in spokes.

Fig. 184. A man-drawn cart
(Reader's Digest Editors *People* 1981, 122).

Fig. 185. A biblical cart
The solid wheels were made of two or three sections of planking, cut from the center of a log. The outer, soft sapwood, which wore down rapidly, was removed before the planks were shaped, and wood battens held the hard wood together (Reader's Digest Editors People *1981, 122).*

Solid wheel

Linch pin

Cross-bar wheel

Spoked wheel

Felloe or Rim

Nave

Fig. 186. Types of ancient wooden wheels

The Egyptians made rims of leather, which were connected with leather thongs. The cart itself was streamlined into a mobile firing platform, built for speed, and was light enough to be carried by two men over rough terrain. Some were outfitted with quivers; bow cases, sheaths, and stands for axes and spears.

The chariot may have reached its peak with the Assyrian army of Ashurbanipal (885-860 B.C.). Their large-wheeled vehicles carried four soldiers: a driver, an archer, and two shield bearers.

The cart also was developed for nonmilitary uses. An ox-drawn wagon could transport heavy loads of produce or equipment and was widely used in agrarian cultures. Oxen usually pulled in pairs, attached to the cart by yoke and pole. Since oxen have minor humps at the withers, a yoke fits them well. Horses, shaped differently, required another arrangement. The flexible throat harness used with oxen gave way to a stiff collar, which would not ride up on the horse's neck, but put pressure on the shoulders and chest of the animal (Landels 1978, 174; Reader's Digest Editors *People* 1981, 45). The harness connected to shafts that ran beside the animal and back to the cart, ensuring equal pull on both sides.

Fig. 187. An Egyptian chariot

The chassis was made of a light wooden frame, designed to carry two or three warriors. Wheels were made of bentwood. Elm, oak, and ash composed the hub, spokes, and felly, respectively.

Fig. 188. Section through two carts, showing alternate assemblies

A linchpin upon a fixed, stub axle holds the wheel at the left, while the wheel at the right is fixed to a rotating axle. Parts of the wheel include the hub, spokes, and felly, with rims of steel or copper. The axle supports the cart and stake rails (Landels 1978, 182).

Fig. 189. Pair of oxen pulling a cart with a block

Fig. 190. Four-ox team with wagon

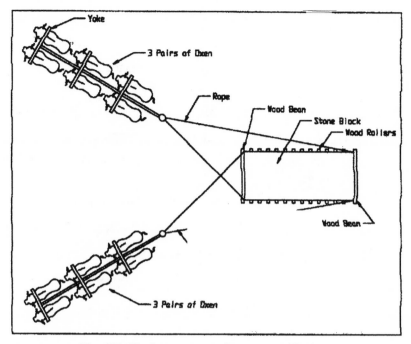

Fig. 191. Twelve oxen moving a stone block

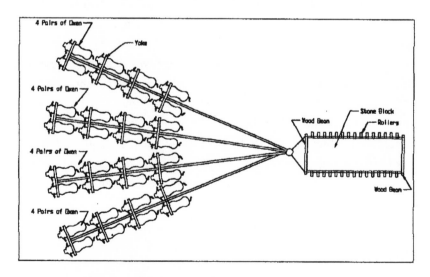

Fig. 192. Thirty-two oxen moving a stone block

Fig. 193. Ox teams pulling stone blocks

In general, ox-drawn carts carried cargo; horse-drawn carts carried passengers. It was strength versus speed. The same idea held true of wheel design. The heavier ox-drawn wagons often had solid wheels or a simple design of crisscrossed planks, while passenger carriages used lighter wheels with spokes. Carts could have either two or four wheels. Oxen fared well with two-wheeled carts, as long as the load remained balanced.

In lighter vehicles, wheels generally rotated on a fixed axle. A short stub of the axle protruded beyond the wheel, and a linchpin kept the wheel from falling off. To prevent excessive wear, a metal washer sometimes separated the wheel hub from the linchpin. In heavier vehicles, the wheels were fixed on the axle, and the axle rotated within brackets fastened to the bottom of the cart. (See Figure 134.)

Roads

With the development of wheeled vehicles, the quality of roadways became a crucial concern. Single animals might poke along a primitive trail, avoiding ruts and obstacles, but a team of animals pulling a wagon needed smoother, level paths.

For thousands of years, road building merely consisted of clearing away boulders and filling in the larger potholes. Most cities had narrow, muddy streets. A few had some paving of fieldstone slabs, but even these did not allow for drainage of rainwater. Some Greek roads followed the beds of dry rivers and streams. In areas where repeated travel had worn two deep wheel ruts into the dirt road, these ruts were paved with cut stone, switches, and siding. The only problem was that the widths of wagons and chariots varied—from four feet, six inches, to four feet, eleven inches, between the wheels—preventing some vehicles from fitting into the grooves.

At first, paving was reserved for processional avenues. One sacred street in Nebuchadnezzar's Babylon had a base of large, flat bricks set in a mixture of lime, sand, and asphalt. On top of these lay a pavement of limestone flags. During religious processions, wagons rolled through this street, bearing statues of the gods. Paving of sacred ways was common in the ancient world, appearing as early as 1200 B.C. At Ashur, a processional road had grooves in the pavement for the sacred wagons, assuring a smooth, safe ride for the gods (Armytage 1961, 18; Miller 1966, 44, 45).

Fig. 194. Cutaway section through a Roman highway

The sequence of construction includes excavation to a firm
sub-grade, stone-rubble fill, flat slabs set in mortar, a
crushed stone and cement cover, curbs of
cut stone, and flat paving stones
closely fitted together,
forming the finished
pavement.

Josephus mentions that Solomon paved the roads leading to Jerusalem with black stones. These, too, might be considered processional avenues. Yet in Palestine the need for paving did not arise until the tumultuous Persian and Hellenistic periods, when armies carted siege machines back and forth throughout the land.

As with other areas of civil engineering, the Romans took road building to its highest level. From about 400 B.C. to A.D. 200, the Romans built a vast system of roads throughout their empire, covering a total distance of 75,000 miles. Twenty-nine highways radiated out from Rome and connected with numerous other local roads. Many of these streets were paved with several layers of stone. Some of these stones can still be seen today.

Fig. 195. Section through an ancient highway between towns

Fig. 196. A paved road with stone curbs
(Cornfeld 1981, 250).

**Fig. 197. A typical town road as
used between buildings**
(Cornfeld 1981, 250).

Even in Palestine, archaeologists have found long sections of Roman-paved roads, complete with curbstones and milestones. Inscriptions on the mile markers list the name of the emperor, the official in charge of road construction, and the distance in Roman miles from the capital of the local district.

Roman roads were generally built and guarded by Roman soldiers. Rome had a sizable army and enjoyed long stretches of peace. At such times the soldiers became civil servants, carrying out a variety of public works, and the military engineers turned their attention to roads, bridges, and aqueducts (Bateman 1942, 1).

The Romans built their roads with a deep sub-base of compacted rubble, covered with layers of flat stone slabs set in mortar. Then they laid another level of concrete and crushed rock, and on top of this set the final paving of close-fitting stones. The surface of the road was slightly crowned, so water would drain off toward the curbstones (although some roads were inversely crowned, to drain toward the center). In most cases, drainage ditches on each side of the road carried off the rainfall.

The Romans had four distinct kinds of roads, from the one-foot-wide footpath (*semita*) to the eight-foot-wide highway (*via*). The Appian Way, begun in 312 B.C., was one of the first and most famous of the Roman *viae*. The ancient Roman road builders showed a great awareness of the crucial elements of road design: durable pavements, foundations, curbs, drainage, slope, and alignment. Their highways followed straight lines wherever possible, had deep cuts or fills to lessen excessive slopes, and passed over culverts and bridges when waterways had to be crossed.

Most streets in Babylon were either parallel or perpendicular to the river. They were narrow and unpaved. They served for access to the houses but also as a dump for household rubbish excrement and filth. Periodically they would cover the trash with a layer of clay, thereby raising the level of the street. Eventually they had to use ladders to get down to the houses.

Bridges

When King Darius I of Persia defeated Thrace and Macedonia in 512 B.C., he transported his troops over the Bosporus Strait by means of a floating military bridge designed by a Samian engineer, Mandrocies. A generation later, King Xerxes sent Persian troops over the Hellespont on a bridge that was supported by 100 ships.

Fig. 198. A Roman military bridge
This bridge is constructed of braced trestle bents supporting wood beams.

Fig. 199. A Roman pontoon bridge

To provide troops with a way to cross to strategic positions, Roman engineers spanned rivers with bridges built atop boats. Anchoring the small vessels upstream, they made use of the force of the water to keep the vessels heading in the same direction. They tied the boats together with ropes and placed beams and planking on the gunwales to create the floating roadway. During construction, they ferried workmen and materials along the downstream side, on a raft and planking. Bridge abutments were made of wood cribbing.

These feats of engineering, forerunners of the modern military pontoon bridge, changed history. The time and effort saved with a well-placed bridge might give one army a significant tactical advantage.

The Romans knew this. They, too, built temporary military bridges, supported by boats or pontoons anchored in position against the current. For permanent installation, the Romans built arched stone bridges.

In sinking the piers for the arched stone bridges, Roman builders formed the *cofferdam* and drove piles into the riverbed. Once the water was pumped out, the arch building could begin. When the pillar reached the waterline, the cofferdam was moved to the next pier site.

One disadvantage of this type of bridge was that the narrow arches restricted water flow and thus increased the velocity of the water; this in turn intensified the erosion process. Yet a number of Roman bridges have lasted to the present day. One stone-arch bridge still in use spans the Tagus River in Alciintra, Spain. Roman masons used sturdy blocks of granite and no mortar to build the seventeen-foot-high arches. They also put a fortified gateway in the middle of this bridge.

As we have seen, ancient engineering was based on intensive application of simple principles and an abundance of raw materials and cheap labor. The Romans devoted more energy and materials to civil projects than previous empires had. While others had constructed great palaces and tombs, the Romans devoted their efforts to roads, bridges, aqueducts, harbors, and sewers. Succeeding civilizations have benefited.

13

Ships and Harbors

WE HAVE LITTLE INFORMATION FROM ANCIENT TIMES ABOUT THE precise designs and methods of shipbuilding. Perhaps the lore of shipbuilding stayed within certain guilds or families, which passed it on to each new generation by word of mouth. Still, from the many extant descriptions of ships and nautical journeys, we can trace the development of nautical engineering.

Egyptian Vessels

The Egyptians and Babylonians had riverboats long before ships sailed the Mediterranean or Red Sea. The earliest vessels, about 4000 B.C., were papyrus boats propelled by oars or a square sail.

When the Egyptians began crafting wooden boats, they were still lightly built, keel-less vessels with only a few thin ribs. Planks were pinned to one another, rather than to a frame. A few beams ran from gunwale to gunwale, supporting a deck. This type of construction was fine for the peaceful Nile, but not for the Mediterranean, with its storms, harsh waves, and ripping currents.

One Nile boat did, however, manage to transport two obelisks, 100 feet long and weighing 350 tons apiece, from quarry to building site. The boat was so large that each of its steering-control oars weighed five tons. It took twenty-seven smaller boats, bearing thirty oarsmen each, to pull this vessel and its load.

Yet this feat shows that Egyptian engineers knew and used the laws of buoyancy and gravity. The ship's hull had to be large enough so that the weight of the water it displaced was greater than the weight of the ship and its cargo. The upward force of buoyancy would counteract the downward force of the obelisk's (and the ship's) weight.

About 1500 B.C., the Egyptians had merchant ships eighty or ninety feet long. Each wooden vessel had a taut hawser between the bow and stern, to reinforce the hull, since it still had no keel or ribs. When the Egyptians did build a fleet of troop-transport ships to sail the Mediterranean, they strengthened their design considerably. Shipbuilders looped a large hawser around one end of the vessel, carried it across the ship's centerline, and then looped the other end. A stout pole was placed through the strands of the hawser, where it passed over the deck, and was twisted to tighten the rope like a tourniquet. The resulting tension compressed the ship. The hawser served the purpose of a keel and ribs by holding the ship together amid the battering of the waves.

Fig. 200. Various early vessels
A large, oared riverboat (right) was used in Egypt about 2000 B.C.

Fig. 201. An Egyptian riverboat

Unlike most modern boats, this ancient craft had no keel. Instead a huge hawser and harnesses on the centerline of the ship held together its sawn cedar planks with scarfs, which were tied together with rope fasteners. With such a vessel the Egyptians carried huge stone obelisks along the Nile.

Builders also ran a horizontal netting around the upper part of the hull. This worked like a girdle, holding the ship together. Since a single mast required a sturdy keel and frame, the Egyptians used a two-legged mast, which distributed the weight across the hull. A single square sail rode on this double mast, stretched between two horizontal poles. Generally the ship also contained oarsmen, who could propel the vessel when the wind was calm.

Light ships like these proved graceful and fast, but they lacked the strength for extended sea travel.

Reed rafts or skiffs similar to the one shown above are still used in the Lower Euphrates Valley. Workmen built them by tying reeds into bundles and lashing them together. By turning up the ends of the boat, they created a stern and bow. To make the craft more watertight, they could cover it with bitumen.

Egyptians used boats like the one shown below when they ventured into the sea. The rigging served a double purpose, since it held the mast in place and allowed the crew to raise and lower the sail. Once the spar was aloft, they could furl the sail on the boom (Mansir 1981, 9).

Phoenician Ships for Commerce and Warfare

Egyptian sea power waned about 1100 B.C. The Phoenicians took their place, dominating Mediterranean trade for centuries.

The Phoenician city-state of Bybios (now Jubayl) became one of the Mediterranean's great shipping centers. *"Bybios ships,"* as they were called, carried cedar wood from Lebanon to Egypt and returned with papyrus and agricultural produce to ship elsewhere. Phoenician ships sailed as far as North Africa, the west coast of Spain, and even southern England. Their seafaring strength lasted until the time of Alexander (Miller 1978, 362-365).

The Phoenicians used two kinds of ships. The "round" ship, with its rounded hull and a raised prow and stern, was used exclusively for commerce. The larger and sleeker "long" ship measured more than 100 feet in length and could be used for either commerce or war. It had very high decks and curved prows, two banks of oars (sixty in all), two steering oars, and a mast in the center that bore a large, square sail. In war, it might be outfitted with bronze shields and a pointed ram and its bow covered with bronze or iron. The long ship could hold as many as 250 men. The Phoenicians were the first to send a convoy of warships with their merchant fleet.

Fig. 202. A wooden seagoing ship
This typical ancient Phoenician merchant was outfitted with both sails and oars. Generally these ships sailed northward, with the wind, and used oars for going southward, against the wind.

The prophet Ezekiel described the glory of the Phoenician seaport of Tyre:

O mighty seaport city, merchant center of the world, the Lord God speaks. You say, "I am the most beautiful city in all the world." You have extended your boundaries out into the sea; your architects have made you glorious. You are like a ship built of the finest fir from Senir. They took a cedar from Lebanon to make a mast for you. They made your oars from oaks of Bashan. The walls of your cabin are of cypress from the southern coast of Cyprus. Your sails are made of Egypt's finest linens; you stand beneath awnings bright with purple and scarlet dyes from eastern Cyprus. Your sailors come from Sidon and Arvad; your helmsmen are skilled men from Zemer. Wise old craftsmen from Gebal do the calking. Ships come from every land with all their goods to barter for your trade. (Ezekiel 27:3-9 TLB).

The united kingdom of Israel reached its economic and territorial peak in the tenth century B.C., under King Solomon. Solomon shrewdly allied with the Phoenician ruler, King Hiram of Tyre. Using Israelite seaports, Phoenician know-how, Israelite wealth, and Phoenician timber, Solomon built a navy that conducted lucrative trade throughout the known world.

Fig. 203. Section through an Egyptian ship
Many keel-less ships, like this seventy-footer, used only a hawser for support. Cargo was stored on the deck. A single or double mast was mounted amidships. At the left, in the stem, lies a raised platform, which acted as the bridge or poop.

King Solomon also built ships at Ezion Geber, which is near Elath in Edom, on the shore of the Red Sea. And Hiram sent his men—sailors who knew the sea—to serve in the fleet with Solomon's men. They sailed to Ophir and brought back 420 talents of gold, which they delivered, to King Solomon (1 Kings 9:26-28 NIV).

The king had a fleet of trading ships at sea along with the ships of Hiram. Once every three years it returned carrying gold, silver, and ivory, and apes and baboons. (1 Kings 10:22 NIV) The ships of this Israeli-Phoenician fleet probably had high prows and single masts that bore single, rectangular sails; they may also have had one bank of oars on each side. Obviously these vessels could sail great distances.

Fig. 204. A Phoenician round ship

Also known as the Hippo ship or Tarshish ship, this vessel had a square sail reinforced by buntlines attached to the foot of the sail and by loops woven into the fabric.

However, the places they went to are something of a mystery to modern scholars. No one knows for sure where Ophir was; though some have speculated it was East Africa or even Sumatra, and Josephus said it was in India. Tarshish appears often in the Bible, and is usually described as a source of metals such as tin and copper. The word may have meant "metal refinery" in ancient Phoenician and thus might refer to any port with Phoenician smelters. Some scholars have placed Tarshish in Spain (Reader's Digest Editors *People* 1981, 184).

Greek Sailing Innovations

Homer described the vessels of the Trojan War as "hollow ships." These must have been mostly un-decked, except for a small landing that could hold a lookout and a few marines, when the ship went to war.

With both sail and oars, such ships could make the best of any fine weather. If a favorable wind blew, the crew erected the sail, first setting up the mast with two forestays, stepping it, locking it with a wedge, and securing it with a backstay. Once they hoisted the sail, they set it with braces. Then the helmsman took his position, holding the leeward sheet in one hand and the tiller in the other. Some ancient vessels might have also carried a foresail (*artemon*), beneath a slanting bowsprit, to keep the bow downwind.

If the wind failed, the crew pulled oars from under the benches that ran along the gunwales. With leather straps, they attached these to the *tholes* (wooden pins used as oarlocks, which provided a fulcrum against which the oar could work).

But this did not solve every sailing problem; most ancient sailing needed the wind—oars could only take you so far. So ships often sat in port, waiting for the right wind to blow. In bad weather, especially from mid-November to mid-February, when harsh winter storms ruled the Mediterranean, sailing also became dangerous, as shown by Paul's experiences in Acts 27, and a good sailor might rightly fear going to sea.

By 800 B.C., Greek shipbuilders created the fighting vessel that would be state-of-the-art for the next thousand years. Homer's old sea rovers, useful in trading and piracy, were inefficient in battle. The new warship had a high, rounded stern and a straight prow with a strong,

Fig. 205. An ancient hollow ship

pointed ram. This ram changed the face of warfare at sea. No longer
were ships just transporters of archers and spearmen—now the ship itself
was a weapon. The navy with the skill to maneuver ships into attacking
positions emerged victorious. Battle became a matter of precise timing.
A slight miscalculation might be the difference between ramming the
enemy and having your own hull ripped open by the enemy's ram.

But warfare was not left entirely to the ship. The new vessel also
included a fighting platform for archers and spearmen. A deck ran from
stem to stern, but not all the way across from bulwark to bulwark. Space
was left at each side for rowers to work either at or below deck level.
While the ship cruised, the oarsmen sat at deck level, but in battle they
retreated to a more protected position below deck. The opening in the
deck provided ventilation.

As ships grew larger, they needed more power. The answer lay in the
addition of a second bank of oars on each side. The Phoenicians originally
invented the two-bank galley ship, or bireme, but the Greeks developed it
further and used it widely by 500 B.C. (Mansir 1981, 17).

Later, the Greeks and Romans installed a third bank of oars. This required additional manpower, but despite popular conception, the oarsmen were not all slaves. Most were freemen. These amazingly maneuverable triremes could reach a speed of ten knots and spin in tight circles. Yet they were not especially seaworthy. With only an eight-foot freeboard and a three-foot draft, a trireme had trouble in turbulent seas. Sails still carried these ships on the high seas, but in battle, the rowers supplied the power. Some triremes were also equipped with an underwater metal-tipped ram.

Roman Ships

Romans used two major types of sailing crafts: long ships and wide ships. The long ships—triremes and quinqueremes (which had five banks of oars)—were narrow and swift, used mainly for war. The heavy wide ships carried cargo and passengers.

Fig. 206. A Greek pentecenter
This ship consisted of the prow at the bow; a bridge poop, aft; and a mast at mid-ships, supporting lapped boom yards, and stayed by fore and aft braces (Landels 1981, 153).

The Roman navy ruled the Mediterranean, and with Rome's warships patrolling, keeping the peace, sea trade flourished. Merchant vessels from Greece, Phoenicia, and Egypt crossed the Mediterranean unmolested.

The apostle Paul traveled on trading ships, since in his day there were no vessels built specifically for passenger service. Merchant ships routinely took on several dozen passengers.

A typical merchant ship might be 140 feet long, thirty-six feet broad, and thirty-three feet deep—with a capacity of three tons. Its design would enable it to sail close to the wind. The decks were covered, with cabins below. Built of wood, with a simple prow, they may have had a raised aft that inclined toward the center of the ship. Though some used oars, most trade vessels relied on sail power. Early ships had a single square sail on a fixed mast, but during the Roman Empire, two or three triangular sails propelled the vessels (Reader's Digest Editors *People* 1981, 390).

Fig. 207. A bireme or two-banked galley
At the stern, one of a pair of steering oars guides the vessel. Forestays secure the mast to the bow, while brails hold it to the stern. Ropes anchored to both sides of the bow keep the yards in position.

On orders from Emperor Caligula, the Romans once hauled a huge stone obelisk from Egypt on a specially designed ship that held 1,300 tons. Taken from Hieropolis, near Cairo, the monument was barged down the Nile and shipped across the Mediterranean on this special vessel. Then it was barged up the Tiber to Rome, where it was re-erected.

Fig. 208. Section through a trireme or three-banked galley

This fifth-century Athenian vessel shows the principal elements of fighting-ship construction used during the Greek Golden Age. Along the spine of the ship, the keelson provides support from bow to stem. A rib frame surrounded by a plank hull holds the three levels of oarsmen, and a raised platform covers them. Atop the mast, a square sail of sheet linen would be suspended with brails on the lapped yards attached to the mast.

Fig. 209. A large stone anchor

This shaped stone anchor from about 1200 B.C. was found in Caesarea.

Navigation

Once people began to sail beyond the sight of the shore, they needed a way to find out where they were. The earliest navigators may have judged their location from the wind direction or by watching the waves or even the birds.

Eventually, sailors found Polaris, the North Star, also called the pole star. This star did not appear to move. It stayed there, always in the north, a true guide for navigators.

**Fig. 210. An ancient mag-
netic compass**
*Early magnetic compasses
like this one, used in the Far
East, consisted of a clay
bowl containing water upon
which floated a thin leaf of
magnetized iron (or lode-
stone) shaped like a fish. The
head of the fish would
always point to magnetic
north (Institute of History
1983, 154).*

The Phoenicians learned to measure their position with their hands. Extending an arm, the ancient navigator lined up his little finger with the horizon and his thumb with the zenith. With certain calculations, he could judge his direction and latitude. Possibly about 150 B.C., Hipparchus invented the astrolabe. Literally meaning a "star taker," the astrolabe measured the angle of the stars above the horizon. With this, a sailor could determine nautical position. Hipparchus's invention consisted of a movable pointer fixed to the center of a wood or metal disk, which had its circumference marked off in degrees. This was the predominant navigational instrument until the sextant was invented.

Navigators probably probed the sea bottom with a sounding pole or a tallow-tipped lead and line, to determine the depth and nature of the sea floor. For instance, Herodotus wrote in the fifth century B.C., "When you get eleven fathoms and ooze on the lead, you are a day's journey from Alexandria" (Casson 1959, 68).

Two thousand years before Columbus sailed to America, Pythagoras altered man understands of navigation when he proclaimed that the earth was round. Later, both Plato and Aristotle would reassert this theory. In the third century B.C., Eratosthenes determined the circumference of the earth to be 25,000 miles, by using fairly simple geometric calculations. In the second century A.D., Claudius Ptolemy laid out the first terrestrial coordinates, the parallels of latitude and the meridians of longitude. The parallels measure the distance from the equator in degrees, up to 90 degrees at the poles. The meridians determine east-west position, measured in degrees (up to 360) from a fixed "prime" meridian. With Ptolemy's coordinates, navigators could more precisely plot their position at sea.

Harbors

Because early ships could not travel long distances at one stretch, numerous ports were established around the Mediterranean. As sea trade flourished, many ports became significant economic centers.

These cities needed efficient harbor facilities to welcome ships and their commerce. Building harbors was, in many cases, as important as the construction of fortresses. Harbor design required not only solid engineering knowledge, but also an awareness of the tides and the destructive effect of the waves (Morgan 1960, 162).

One of the most ancient ports on Palestine's coast, Joppa (or Jaffa) bears the remains of numerous civilizations. Excavators have found fortifications from the Bronze Age right on through to Byzantine and Arab times.

Into Joppa's port came the cedars of Lebanon that Solomon used for the Temple construction (2 Chronicles 2:16). King Hiram's workers floated them down to the sea on barges. At Joppa, Jonah boarded the ship for

Tarshish, running away from Nineveh, where God had ordered him to go.

Acco (also called Acre or Ptolemais) was another major port of Palestine. North of Caesarea, but south of Tyre, it served the Jezreel Valley and the region of Galilee. Through Acco passed the major highway from Egypt, the Via Maris, and east-west roads through Jezreel connected Acco with the other major thoroughfare, the King's Highway.

Gaza, in the south, originally served as a key caravan point between Egypt and the rest of the Middle East. After the Romans rebuilt the city closer to the shore, this harbor became a major port of embarkation for eastern merchants.

Tyre was once an island, one-half mile from shore. In 332 B.C., the army engineers of Alexander the Great built a land bridge or causeway so they could bring their siege engines to the city walls. Over time, silt has accumulated on this land bridge to form the present neck of land, 600 yards across at its narrowest point. Both Tyre and its sister city, Sidon, have small islands and reefs offshore that function as breakwaters, creating a peaceful inner harbor.

Caesarea, however, emerged as the most magnificent port built on Palestine's coast. Originally known as Strato's Tower, named for a Phoenician king, Herod renamed it to honor the emperor. He spared no expense in making this a world-class seaport.

Since Caesarea had no natural harbor, Herod's engineers built a 200-foot-wide breakwater for docking and anchoring vessels; it also protected the inner harbor from the ravages of waves and currents from the southwest. To the north, a semicircular seawall enclosed a marina of sorts—a yacht basin with an entrance—guarded by two immense, statue-bearing towers.

The northern breakwater measured an estimated 250 yards; the southern one 600 yards. The enclosed area measured about forty acres. In his *War of the Jews,* Josephus described the construction of Caesarea:

> *After Herod had marked out the comparative dimensions of the harbor . . .*
> *he had blocks of stone sunk into twenty fathoms of sea-most of which were*
> *fifty-feet long, nine deep and ten broad, some being even larger. When these*
> *submarine foundations had risen to the water level he built above the sur-*

face a mole 200 feet wide; one hundred of these are built out into the sea to break the force of the waves and, therefore, called the breakwater, while the remainder supported the stone wall that encircled the harbor. Massive towers are spaced at intervals above this wall and the most conspicuous and magnificent is called Drusiurn after Caesar's stepson, Drusas (Whiston 1979, 162).

Apparently, the builders began by digging out the inner harbor and piers. Once they had excavated the outer harbor, they removed the narrow strip of land separating the two harbors, allowing water into the inner basins.

Fig. 211. Harbor at Caesarea

At the bottom of the harbor stands a mastery of harbor-building technology that rivals present-day knowledge. At several points, a sluice system enabled sand-free water from the open sea into the enclosed harbor. This created circulation within the enclosed basins and inhibited silting. A subsidiary breakwater system protected the main enclosing arm of the harbor at its most vulnerable point.

These builders also made great use of the new hydraulic concrete that hardened underwater, becoming practically impervious to the sea's destructive force. At Caesarea, archaeologists have found blocks of hydraulic concrete weighing fifty tons. They measure fifty feet by nine feet by ten feet, even larger than those Josephus described.

Completed in 9 B.C., the city had a population of 40,000 by the second century A.D. Caesarea was the first port in Palestine that could provide anchorage for as many as one hundred Roman war galleys. The moles contained buildings that served as dormitories for sailors and warehouses and had walkways where people could enjoy the sea breeze. A tall tower served as a lighthouse.

In A.D. 130, an earthquake damaged the harbor, and by the fourth or fifth century A.D., it had become unusable.

Trade and the Biblical World

Not until the reigns of Solomon and Jehoshaphat did the Israelites develop extensive land and sea trade routes. These two kings, who ruled almost a hundred years apart, utilized Israel's central geographic position as the land bridge between ports on the Mediterranean and Ezion geber on the Red Sea. But after neighboring powers conquered them, the Hebrews lost access to the ports and relied on land travel by caravan.

The conquest of Jaffa by the Hasmonaeans again provided the Judean kingdom with access to the sea routes when this port was opened to Greek merchants, who replaced the Phoenicians. Jaffa's port again became an important center of international commerce.

During the Roman period, trans-Mediterranean trade was controlled by the Roman fleet. Their large and strong merchant ships carried soldiers, goods, merchants, and passengers; some of the apostles traveled to and from Judea. Judea become part of the Roman commercial complex. Nabataean trade, carried by camel trains, crossed southern Palestine, carrying spices, perfumes, herbs, precious woods, and gems from the Far East and southern Arabia to Gaza and other ports on the Mediterranean. By land and sea, the Holy Land continued to serve as the hub from which culture, knowledge, and religion spread throughout the region.

Glossary

Acanthus leaves Architectural ornaments used in capitals of Corinthian and composite orders, representing the foliage of the acanthus plant.

Acco (also known as Acre and Ptolemais) For centuries the best and most important harbor in northern Palestine, it was a major stop on the main north-south highway, the Via Maris.

Adobe Natural, sun-dried clays with a binder.

Adze An ax-type tool used in chipping the surface of wood. Its cutting edge is perpendicular to the axis of the handle.

Akkadia Ancient Mesopotamian city built by Nimrod in northern Babylonia.

Altar A place of sacrifice, built of a heap of stones and earth. Some altars were even made of acacia wood and overlaid with bronze.

Amorite People descended from the fourth son of Canaan. They made up the pre-Canaanite population of Palestine.

Amphiprostyle A building with columnar porches at both ends but without a peristyle.

Antonia Fortress A structure at the north side of the Temple Mount, built by Herod the Great.

Aqueduct A raised masonry structure containing a channel for carrying water from a source at a higher elevation.

Arcade A series of arches supported by piers and columns, or a covered passageway.

Arch A structure composed of separate wedge-shaped stones or bricks arranged in a curved line, so as to retain their position by mutual pressure.

Architrave The main long horizontal beam supported by the upper slab of the column capitals, which replaced the wood beams.

Ark A decorated chest in which the Tablets of the Covenant were kept.

Ark, Noah's a vessel built by Noah for saving his family's lives during the Great Flood.

Artemon A small sail attached to the long spar forward of the bow, used to keep a ship before the wind and as a steering aid.

Ashlar masonry Masonry constructed of square-hewn stone.

Assault tower A wooden structure used to provide access to the top of a fortress wall or to support a battering ram for breaking through the wall.

Assyria An ancient and powerful kingdom in Mesopotamia.

Astrolabe An ancient instrument, said to be invented by Hipparchus in 150 B.C., used for taking the altitude of the sun or stars at sea. The quadrant and sextant replaced it when navigational technology advanced.

Awl A pointed tool used to chop wood. It has a wooden handle and a bronze or iron blade. A small boring tool.

Babel A great city built in the Plains of Shimr.

Ballista A siege engine that propels stones or iron darts.

Barrel vault A masonry, arch-like structure.

Battering ram An ancient offensive engine of war used to beat down walls of besieged places. It consists of a large pole, with a head of iron shaped to resemble the head of a ram.

Battlement A fortress, or a notched or indented parapet of a tower or wall used for defense.

Bireme An ancient Greek or Roman galley with two banks of oars, originally developed by the Phoenicians.

Bitumen Asphalt or tar.

Block A pulley used with ropes and tackle, consisting of a slim oval shell of wood. Inside, ropes run around one or more sheaves (pulley wheels).

Bloom Semi-plastic molten iron. Brass An alloy of copper and zinc. In biblical usage the word brass signified copper or bronze.

Breakwater A structure protecting a shore area, harbor, anchorage, or basin from the waves.

Bronze A metal made from an alloy of copper and tin.

Bronze Age A historical period characterized by the use of bronze for tools and weapons.

Buttress A structure built against or projecting from a wall or building for the purpose of giving it stability.

Byblos A port of ancient Lebanon.

Byzantine Pertaining to Byzantium, an ancient city, later called Constantinople, which became the capital of the Eastern Roman Empire.

Caesar The title used for the Roman emperors from Augustus to Hadrian, later applied to the heir presumptive.

Caesarea Originally known as Strato's Tower, Herod the Great built it into a thriving port. The port was known for its extensive breakwaters and harbor facilities.

Capital The head or cornice of a columns.

Canaan Part of ancient Palestine, between Jordan, the Dead Sea, and the Mediterranean; the land God promised to Abraham.

Capstan Mechanism used for hoisting blocks or cargo, consisting of a vertical axle,

drum, toothed wheel, and pawls fixed to the axle, which engage the toothed wheel to prevent a cable from running backward in the absence of pressure on the levers.

Casemate wall Two parallel walls, a heavy outer wall and a lighter inner wall, connected by cross walls, which form chambers, or casemates, between the two walls. As an added defense, these chambers were sometimes filled with stones.

Catapult A siege engine for throwing pikes or stones. A large crossbow mounted on a pedestal shot darts up to six feet in length. Also known as quick-firers.

Causeway A street or highway, a raised road across wet or marshy ground or across water.

Centering Shoring for construction of arches.

Chariot A two- or four-wheeled cart pulled by horses and used in warfare.

Cistern A manmade reservoir that is filled with rainwater or water brought from springs.

Citadel A fortress or castle.

Cherub An angelic being illustrated in ancient art

with a woman's head on a winged lion's body.

Cofferdam An angelic being illustrated in ancient art with a woman's head on a winged lion's body.

Colonnade A series of columns placed at regular intervals and used to support a roof structure.

Conduit A pipe, tube, or channel used for conveyance of water.

Corbeling An overlapping arrangement of stones, in which each course projects beyond the one below.

Corinthian order A style of Greek or Roman architecture decorated with acanthus leaves.

Cornice The uppermost member of an entablature, resting on a frieze.

Counterpoise A counterbalancing weight.

Coarse Rubble Masonry work made of undressed stones of irregular size.

Coursed masonry Masonry work laid in horizontal planes.

Crane A lifting apparatus for raising blocks or cargo.

Crenelated walls A fortress wall with openings

through which defenders could shoot on those below.

Crete Also known as Cheretim, the largest and southernmost of the Greek islands, from which the Philistines may have originated.

Crossbow A weapon formed by placing a bow perpendicularly on the stock, from which arrows are released.

Cubit A biblical unit of measurement, 1 foot, 6 inches, or 1 foot, 9 3/8 inches; the length of the lower arm from the elbow to the tip of the middle finger.

Cut stones Stones with smoothly dressed beds and joints.

Cyclopean masonry Rubble masonry made with very large, irregular rock.

Dagan Philistine's fertility god.

Dart thrower A type of catapult.

Debir The Holy of Holies of the Jerusalem Temple, Inner sanctuary.

Dentils A series of small, rectangular blocks, protruding like rows of teeth, as under a cornice.

Derrick An apparatus used for hoisting and lowering weights, comprised of a boom secured at the foot of the mast, from which runs a block and tackle, controlling the elevation and traverse of the boom.

Displacement The weight of a vessel based on Archimedes' principle that it equals the weight of water displaced by its hull.

Divided Kingdom The period of Hebrew history from 928 B.C. to 586 B.C., ending with the destruction of the state of Judah and the Babylonian Exile.

Dome A hemispheric roof constructed of shaped stones.

Dome of the Rock An Islamic structure built on the Temple Mount. Mosque of Omar.

Doric Order A style of Greek or Roman architecture.

Draft The depth of a vessel from the keel to the waterline.

Eggs-and-darts An architectural ornamentation.

Elath (Eloth) A port on the Gulf of Elath.

Engines of war Ancient artillery, machines used to hurl arrows, spears, and stones, including catapults and testudos.

Erez Israel Land of Israel.

Ethrog Citron fruit.

Extrados The exterior curve or surface of an arch or vault.

Ezion geber A port at the southern point of Palestine, where Solomon's ships, built with Tyrian help, took part in independent maritime commerce.

Fathom A unit of measurement of water depth, equal to six feet, or 1.83 meters.

Fiber rope Ropes made from pine-tree bark, coconut hair, camel hair, horsehair, thongs cut from hide, cotton, jute, sisal, flax, or hemp.

Finger A unit of measurement, .7 or .9 inch.

Forecastle The forward deck, which is raised above the main deck. It was used as a fighting "castle" by soldiers carried on board the ships.

Frieze The part of an entablature of a column that is between the architrave and the cornice.

Froutin A Roman engineer (A.D. 40-103) who built aqueducts in Rome.

Fulcrum The point of support by which a lever is sustained.

Galil Galilee.

Galley An ancient sail-and or oar-propelled vessel.

Gangue Impurities in iron making.

Gastraphete The belly weapon, a type of cross-bow.

Gate post The post upon which a gate swings or the one against which it closes.

Gaza Town on the southwest coast of Palestine. It was an important caravan point en route to Egypt.

Gneiss A metamorphic rock similar to granite.

Glacis A sloping bank or defensive wall used against battering rams and to make approach more difficult. It also effectively ricocheted stones dropped by the defenders.

Granary A structure or pit used to store grain.

Grapnel A hooked device used to fasten and hold one ship to another.

Greek fire A flammable mixture of naphtha, sulfur, and pitch used in warfare.

Groined vault; A structure made by the intersection of two barrel vaults.

Gunwale The upper edge of a ship's side.

Gypsos Greek word for plaster.

Gypsum A mineral ($CaSO4$- $2H20$) used to make plaster.

Hand A unit of measurement equal to four fingers.

Hasmonaeans The family name of the priestly family popularly known as the Maccabees.

Hekel or Hechal Main hall of Temple.

Hittites An ancient people who flourished in the eastern Mediterranean area for about seven centuries before 1200 B.C.

Holy of Holies The inner chamber of the sanctuary of the Jewish Temple.

Igneous rock Original rock including granite, basalt, and diorite.

In antis With a porch having two or more columns enclosed between projecting side walls of a celia (a windowless structure).

Intrados The interior curve of an arch. Ionic order A style of Greek or Roman architecture.

Iron Age A period, about 1200 B.C., in which use of iron superseded bronze.

Joppa A port, also known as Jaffa, where Solomon brought timbers shipped from Lebanon on barges and had them hauled up to Jerusalem (2 Chronicles 2:16).

Josephus A Jewish historian, public official, and general (A.D. 37-100). He was also called Flavius Josephus.

Keel The backbone of a ship, from which the ribs project.

Kiln A type of oven used to bake or dry clay or brick.

KJV King James Version of the Bible

Knot A unit of speed used in navigation, equal to one nautical mile (6,076.115 feet or 1,852 meters) per hour.

Lanyard The rope trigger of a siege engine, catapult, or artillery.

Lepis Albanas Sperona, peperino.

Lepis Tiburtinus Travertine.

Lime Calcium oxide (CaO), a white, caustic solid made by calcining limestone and other calcium carbonate substances. It is used for mortar and cement.

Limestone A rock consisting chiefly of calcium carbonate.

Lime plaster Plaster made of dehydrated, crushed limestone.

Lintel The beam over a door or window opening.

Long ship A large, streamlined ancient Phoenician ship. (See also Trireme and Quinquereme.)

Luller; Palm branches

Mason One who hews stones into shape for construction.

Menorah A seven-branched candelabrum.

Meridian A longitude line, a circle drawn around the earth, through the poles.

Milestone A cylindrical, inscribed stone placed along the highway by the Romans. It describes the emperor authorizing the construction of the road, the person in charge of construction, and the distance in Roman miles to the capital of the district.

Military engineer A soldier whose specialty is building and destroying military structures.

Moabites People of Moab, an ancient nation in the Transjordan.

Mole In coastal terminology, a massive land-connected, solid-fill structure of earth, (generally revetted) masonry, or large stone that serves as a breakwater or pier.

Mortar A mixture of lime, sand, ash, and water, used for plastering cisterns and reservoirs to make them water resistant. It is also used as a binder in masonry.

Mount of Olives A hill on the east side of the Temple Mount.

NEB New English Bible.

Nimrod A warrior who established the kingdom of Babylonia and later extended into Assyria.

Nineveh, Assyrian capital ancient city founded by Nimrod in north Mesopotamia and the capital of the Assyrian Empire in 705-612 B.C.

NIV New International Version.

Obelisk An ancient Egyptian stone monument.

Onager catapult A large siege machine, based on torsion, with a lever that pulled back against a tightly twisted rope of fiber, sinew, or hair. It was named after the wild ass because of its kick.

Parallels Lines of latitude. The distance north and south of the equator, measured in degrees, from 0 at the equator to 90 at the poles.

Pax Romana A two-century period of Roman prosperity, beginning in 27 B.C.

Pentecenter An ancient Greek sailing ship.

Peristyle A structure surrounded by columns.

Persia A country inhabited by the Indo-Europeans from Russia into the Iranian plains in 1000 B.C.

Philistines People of Philistia, the plain extending south of the Mt. Carmel along the Mediterranean Sea to Gaza.

Philistia An ancient country on the southwest coast of Palestine.

Phoenicia Ancient Lebanon.

Pila A thrusting spear.

Pillar A vertical stone structure used to support or a column.

Pitch A viscous substance used for waterproofing. It is made from coal, tar, asphalt, or wood resin.

Plaster Mortar or cement used as a coating over clay or stone wall or as a binder between bricks and blocks. In Palestine, the material commonly used was clay, in the Euphrates Valley, slime (or bitumen).

Polaris The north or polar star, by which navigators could figure their position.

Portico A kind of porch fronted with columns, often at the entrance of a building.

Post and lintel A type of structure involving two columns and a beam (or lintel).

Pozzolana A volcanic ash or powdered rock used by the Romans to make hydraulic cement.

Prostyle Having columnar porches at both ends, but no peristyle.

Proto-aeolic The original or first.

Ptolemaic Period The era of the Greek philosopher Ptolemy or the Ptolemies, kings of ancient Egypt.

Pulley One of the simple machines for raising weights, consisting of a small wheel that moves around an axle and has a groove cut in its circumference, through which a cord runs.

Quay A harbor structure, stretch of paved bank, or solid, artificial landing place parallel to a navigable waterway, for use in loading and unloading ships.

Quick firer A type of catapult. (See also Catapult.)

Quinquereme A galley with five banks of oars.

Ram A siege machine used for battering down fortress walls. (See also Battering ram.)

Ram tortoise A wheeled shed, or tortoise, with a battering ram suspended on chains hung from the roof.

Rigging Ropes and other equipment used for hoisting and bracing of poles.

Rise The vertical height of an arch, between the spring line and the crown.

Rubble masonry A wall made of uncut stones.

Sand lime A mixture of sand and lime, used as mortar.

Sapper A soldier in the engineering corps who is trained in fortifications.

Saw Ancient saws were long flint knives with jagged edges or bits of flint fitted into a wooden frame.

Scorpion A type of catapult.

Semicircular arch An arch of less than 180 degrees.

Semita A Roman footpath.

Sextant An instrument for measuring angles of heavenly bodies from the horizon. Used in navigation.

Sidon A port town on the coast of Lebanon.

Siege tower A tall structure used to attack a city or fortress. The height gave archers a chance to fire down upon defenders. Some siege towers also carried battering rams.

Skein Twisted fibers of hair or rope.

Skewback A sloping surface that supports the end of an arch.

Sling An offensive weapon used by hunters or shepherds against wild beasts and in warfare.

Spring line The horizontal line at the base of an arch.

Stele An upright slab or pillar, usually with an inscription.

Strato's Tower See Caesarea.

Sumer The ancient name of Babylonia.

Synagogue A Jewish place of worship and house of assembly.

Tabernacle The tent in which Hebrews worshiped in the presence of God and which was taken with them on their journeys in the wilderness.

Talent A weight equivalent to 47 or 48 pounds.

Tar A distillation of wood or coal employed to waterproof wood, textiles, yarns, or rope.

Tarshish A biblical city from which copper was obtained.

Testudos "Turtles," catapults that hurled flaming spears.

Tin A metal used, along with copper, to make bronze.

Torsion machine A siege weapon such as an onager.

Tortoise A type of siege engine.

Trebuchet A type of catapult.

Trireme A battleship containing three banks or tiers of oars, used by the Greeks and Romans.

Tufa A soft, tan volcanic rock.

Tyre A port city on coast of Lebanon.

Ulam The outer chamber of the Jewish Temple.

United Kingdom The period from last days of David, 973 B.C. to 933 B.C., when the Israelite kingdom was divided.

Unsquared Stone Stone that is used as it comes from the quarry, without any preparation other than removal of very acute angles and excessive projections.

Ur Native city of Abraham in south Babylonia.

Vault An arched structure, made of stones, forming a ceiling or roof.

Via A Roman highway.

Via Maris A Roman highway in ancient Palestine.

Vitruvius Roman engineer-architect of the first century A.D.

Volute A spiral, scroll-like, or twisted formation, a distinctive feature of the Ionic column.

Voussoirs Any of the pieces in the shape of a truncated wedge that form an arch or vault.

Watchtower A fortified structure on the wall or above the gate of a city.

Windlass A hoisting or hauling apparatus consisting of a horizontal drum on which is wound a rope, attached to the object to be raised or moved. Used to weigh anchors on ancient ships, it was smaller than a capstan and operated on a vertical axis.

Yahweh God.

Ziggurat A stepped Babylonian temple.

Bibliography

Allsopp, Bruce. *A General History of Architecture*. London: Sir Isaac Pittman & Sons, 1965.

Armytage, W. H. G. *A Social History of Engineering*. London: Faber & Faber, 1961.

Archer, Fischler & Wyke, *Women in Ancient Societies*, London: Macmillan, 1994.

Aumann, Moshe, and others, ed. *Carta's Historic Atlas of Israel: A Survey of the Past and Review of the Present*. Jerusalem: Carta (Publishing), *nd*.

Avid, Nahman. *Discovering Jerusalem*. Jerusalem: Shikmona Publishing Co. Ltd., 1980.

Avierzir, Nathan. *In the Beginning*, Hoboken, NJ: Ktav Publishing House, 1990.

Babbitt, Harold E. and James Dolland. *Water Supply Engineering*. New York: McGraw-Hill, 1939.

Bahat, Dan, ed. *Carta's Historic Atlas of Jerusalem*. Jerusalem: Carta (Publishing), 1992.

Bailey, Albert Edward. *Daily Life in Bible Times*. New York: Scribner, 1982.

Bateman, John A. *Introduction to Highway Engineering*. London: John Wiley & Sons, 1942.

Ben-Dov, Jeruslaem. *Man and Stone*. Tel Aviv: Modan Publishing House, 1990.

Ben-Sasson, H. H. *A History of the Jewish People*. Cambridge, MA: Harvard UP, 1976.

Brown, Curtis Maitland. *Evidence and Procedures of Boundary Location*. New York: John Wiley & Sons, 1962.

Bruce, F. F. *New Testament History*, Doubleday-Galilee, Garden City, NY: Doubleday, 1971.

Canaan, Gershon. *Rebuilding the Land of Israel*. New York: Architectural Book Publishing Co., 1954.

Casson, Lionel. *The Ancient Mariners*. New York: Macmillan, 1959.

——— *Ships and Seamanship in the Ancient World*. Princeton, NJ: Princeton University Press, 1971.

Chellis, Robert D. *Pile Foundations*. New York: McGraw-Hill, 1961.

Cornfeld, Galalya. *Archaeology of the Bible: Book by Book*. San Francisco: Harper and Row, 1976.

——— *Josephus: The Jewish War*. Grand Rapids: Zondervan, 1982.

De Camp, L. Sprague. *The Ancient Engineers*. New York: Ballantine, 1959.

——— *The Ancient Engineers*. New York: Doubleday, 1963.

Derry, T. K. and William Trever I. *A Short History of Technology*. New York: Oxford UP, 1960.

Duncan-Jones, Richard. *The Economy of the Roman Empire, Quantitative Studies*. 2nd ed. New York: Cambridge UP, 1982.

Fletcher, Banister. *A History of Architecture*. London: Scribner, 1950.

Ferrill, Arthur. *The Origins of War*. London: Thames and Hudson, 1985.

Geuthner, Paul. *Revue d'Art Oriental et d'Archeologie*. Libraire Orientaliste, 1977.

Gilber, Martin. *The Arab-Israeli Conflict: Its History in Maps*. 3d ed. London: Weidenfeld & Nicolson, 1979.

Granger, F. *The Ten Books of Vitruvius*. Cambridge, MA: Harvard UP, 1988.

Hamlin, A. D. *A Textbook of the History of Architecture*. London: Longmans, Green & Co., 1904.

Hamlin, Talbot. *Architecture through the Ages*. G.P. Putnam's Sons, NY 1940.

Hodges, Henry. *Technology in the Ancient World*. New York: Knopf, 1974.

Isaacson, Ben. *Dictionary of Jewish Religion*. Englewood, NJ: SBS Publishing, 1979.

Jones, R. H. and Peter Brunt, ed. *The Roman Economy*. Oxford, Blackwell, 1974.

Keel, Othmar. *The Symbolism of the Biblical World*. New York: Seabury Press, 1978.

Kemp, Peter. *The History of Ships*. London: Orbis Publishing, 1978.

Kenyon, Kathleen M. *Jerusalem: Excavating 3000 Years of History*. London: Thames and Hudson, 1967.

Kollek, Teddy and Moshe Pearlman. *Jerusalem: Sacred City of Mankind*. Jerusalem: Steinmetzky's Agency, 1974.

Kolatch, Alfred. *The Jewish Book of Why*. New York: Jonathan David Publishers, 1981.

Kutcher, Arthur. *The New Jerusalem: Planning and Politics*. London: Thames and Hudson, 1973.

Landels, J. G. *Engineering in the Ancient World*. Los Angeles: University of California Press, 1981.

Lockyer, Herbert. *All the Trades and Occupations of the Bible*, Grand Rapids: Zondervan, 1969.

Macaulay, David. *City: A Study of Roman Planning and Construction*. Boston: Houghton Mifflin, 1974.

————— *Pyramid*. Boston: Houghton Mifflin, 1975.

Menen, Aubrey. *Cities of the Sand*. London: Thames & Hudson, 1972.

Mansir, A. Richard. *A Modeler's Guide to Ancient and Medieval Ships*. Dana Point, CA: Monraker Publications, 1981.

Mazar, Benjamin. *Mountain of the Lord*. Garden City, NY: Doubleday, 1975.

Merriman, Thaddeus. *American Civil Engineer's Handbook*. London: John Wiley & Sons, 1947.

Miller, John Anderson. *Atoms and Epochs*. Boston: Twayne Publishers, 1966.

Miller, Madelaine S. and J. Lane Miller. *Harper's Encyclopedia of Bible Life*. New York: Harper and Rowe, 1971.

Morgan, Morris Hicky. *Vitruvius: The Ten Books of Architecture*. New York: Dover, 1960.

National Geographic Society. *The Builders: Marvels of Engineering*. 1992.

Negev, Avraham. *Archaeological Encyclopedia of the Holy Land*. Englewood, NJ: SBS Publishing, 1980.

Oleson, John Peter. *Greek and Roman Mechanical Water Lifting Devices: The History of Technology*. Boston: Reidel, 1984.

Paul, Shalom Paul and William G. Dever. *Biblical Archaeology*. Jerusalem: Keter Publishing House, 1973.

Ramsey, Charles George and Harold Reeve Sleeper. *Architectural Graphic Standards*. 5th ed. New York: John Wiley & Sons, 1961.

Readers Digest Editors. *Great People of the Bible*. Pleasantville, NY: Readers Digest Association, 1981.

————— *Atlas of the Bible*. Pleasantville, NY: Readers Digest Association, 1981.

—————— *Story of the Bible World*. Pleasantville, NY: Readers Digest Association, 1962.

—————— *Quest for the Past*. Pleasantville, NY: Readers Digest Association, 1984.

Reich, Hanns. *Jerusalem*. New York: Hill and Wang, 1969.

Reid, Richard. *The Book of Buildings*. New York: Van Nostrand Reinhold, 1983.

Rossnagel, W. E. *Handbook of Rigging*. New York: McGraw-Hill Book Co., 1964.

Rowland, Ingrid and Thomas Nobel Howe. *The Ten Books of Vitruvius*. New York: Cambridge UP, *nd*.

Sed-Rajna, Gabrielle. *Ancient Jewish Art*. Chartwell Books, Inc.

Schiffman, Lawrence H. *From Text to Tradition: A History of Second Temple & Rabbinical Judaism*, Hoboken, NJ: Ktav Publishing House, 1991.

—————— *Texts and Traditions: A Source Reader for the Study of Second Temple and Rabbinical Judaism*. Hoboken, NJ: Ktav Publishing House, 1998.

Schwartz, Max. *Machines, Buildings, and Weaponry of Biblical Times*. Old Tappan, NJ: Fleming H. Revell, 1990.

Sitchin, Zecharia. *The 12th Planet*. New York: Avon Books, 1978.

—————— *Genesis Revisited*. New York: Avon Books, 1990.

Siegner, Otto. *This is Greece*. New York: Munich-Pullach, 1982.

Silberman, Neil Asher. *Digging for God and Country*. New York: Alfred A. Knopf, 1982.

Smith and Engleburg. *Egyptian Masonry*.

Smith, David Eugene. *History of Mathematics*. New York: Dover Publications, Inc., *nd*.

Straub, Hans. *A History of Civil Engineering*. Cambridge: M.I.T. Press, 1962.

Tevor, Moshe. *Jerusalem*. New York: Hill & Wang, 1989.

Thubron, Colin. *Jerusalem*. Amsterdam: Time-Life Books, 1976.

Time-Life Books. *The Great Cities: Jerusalem*. Amsterdam: Time-Life Books, 1976.

Watson, G. R. *The Roman Soldier*. Ithaca, NY: Cornell UP, 1969.

Wheeler, Mortimer. *Splendors of the East: Temples, Tombs, Palaces and Fortresses of Asia*. New York: Spring Books, 1965.

Whiston, William. *The Works of Flavius Josephus: The Wars of the Jews*. Grand Rapids: Baker Book House, 1979.

—————— *Josephus: Complete Works*. Grand Rapids: Kregel Publications, 1981.

White, K. D. *Greek and Roman Technology*. Ithaca, NY: Cornell UP, 1984.

Whitehouse & Wilkens. *The Making of Civilization*. New York: Alfred Knopf, 1966.

Wilson, Captain Charles W. *Ordnance Survey of Jerusalem*. London: Lords' Commissioners of Her Majesty's Treasury, 1886.

Winter, F. E. *Greek Fortifications*. Toronto: University of Toronto Press, 1971.

Yadin, Yigdal. *The Art of Warfare in Biblical Lands in the Light of Archaeological Study*. Vols. 1 and 2. New York: McGraw-Hill, 1963.

Yaggy, L. W. and T. L. Haines. *Museum of Antiquity*. Chicago: Western Publishing House, 1881.

Yonah, Avi. *Encyclopedia of Archaeological Excavations in the Holy Land*. Jerusalem: Israel Exploration Society and Masada Press, 1976.

PERIODICAL ARTICLES

Ben-Dov, Meir. "Herod's Mighty Temple Mount." *Biblical Archaeology Review*. Nov/Dec 1986.

Biblical Archaeology Society. "Reconstructing Herod's Temple Mount in Jerusalem."
    Nov/Dec 1989 Vol. XV No. 6.
Biblical Archaeology Society. "Herod's Temple Mount: Stone by Stone." Nov/Dec 1989
    Vol. XV No. 6
Fritz, Volkman. "Temple Architecture: What Can Archaeology Tell Us about Solomon's
    Temple?" *Biblical Archaeology Review*. July/August 1987.
La Perrousaz, Ernest-Marie. "King Solomon's Wall Still Supports the Temple Mount"
    Biblical Archaeology Review. May/June 1987.
Mubley, James D. "How Iron Technology Changed the World and Gave the Philistines a
    Military Edge." *Biblical Archaeology Review*. Nov/Dec 1982.
Netzer, Ehud. "Jewish Rebels Dig Strategic Tunnel System." *Biblical Archaeology
    Review*. July/August 1988.
O'Connor, Leo, "Building a Better Trebuchet." *Mechanical Engineering*, Jan. 1944.
Shanks, Hershel. "Excavating in the Shadow of the Temple Mount." *Biblical
    Archaeology Review*. Nov/Dec 1986.
————— "Ancient: A Short History from Abraham to the Roman Destruction of the
    Temple." Biblical Archaeology Society, 1991.
————— "Ancient Israel." *Biblical Archaeology Review*, 1991.

ADDITIONAL REFERENCE MATERIALS

Academic American Encyclopedia. Grolier Electronic Publishing, 1990.
The Amplified Bible. Grand Rapids: Zondervan, 1965.
Carta's Historical Atlas of Israel. Jerusalem: Carta (Publishing), 1977.
Encyclopedia Judaica. Jerusalem: Keter Publishing House, 1978.
Engineers' Illustrated Thesaurus. New York: Chemical Publishing Co., 1952.
The Holy Scriptures. Chicago: Menorah Press, 1960.
The Holy Bible: Authorized King James Version. Collins World, *nd*.
The Holy Scriptures According to the Masoretic Text. Philadelphia: Jewish Publications
    Society of America, 1963.
Jewish Encyclopedia. Hoboken, NJ: Ktav Publishing House, Inc., 1967.
Living Webster Encyclopedia of the English Language. The English Language Institute
    of America, Chicago, 1977.
New Marked Reference Bible. (King James Version). Grand Rapids: Zondervan, 1978.
Revell Bible Dictionary. Old Tappan, NJ: Fleming H. Revell, 1990.
Webster Encyclopedia Dictionary of the English Language. Chicago: The English
    Language Institute, 1950.

Subject Index

Scripture Index

246

Index of Persons

Index of Places